The Forward Book of Poetry
2023

The Forward Book of Poetry

2023

Forward
Prizes
for Poetry

First published in Great Britain by
Forward Arts Foundation · Somerset House Exchange ·
The Strand · London · WC2R 1LA
in association with
Faber & Faber · Bloomsbury House · 74-77 Great Russell Street
London WC1B 3DA

ISBN 978 0 571 37758 9 (paperback)

Typeset by Avon DataSet Ltd, Alcester, Warwickshire B49 6QA

Printed and bound by CPI Group (UK) · Croydon CR0 4YY

A CIP catalogue reference for this book
is available at the British Library

To you, dear reader –
The Forward Prizes was founded very much with you in mind,
and after two years of disappointments and delays, of separations and
isolations, we are grateful that you have made your way, here.

Contents

The Forward Prize for Best Single Poem
Shortlisted poems

Highly Commended Poems 2022

Foreword

One completely ordinary week, I see two things that surprise me, maybe three. Early in the morning, while running, I see a man sleeping on a hard wooden bench. The sun has risen, but only just. There are warm slivers of light falling on the street, barely touching the day. The man is homeless, he has sneakers on, he has worn them all night, and a rough blanket pulled nearly all the way over his head. His face is pressed against a folded arm and from whatever I can see of him, I see ruin. The red blotches that cover his face, the angry curl of his body, the fist under his cheek. But as I pass him, so does a woman who also sleeps rough around this same bench. I see her sometimes in the morning, wearing bright shirts, her white hair cut short and with style, talking to pigeons or screaming at parked bicycles. Today, she walks over to the sleeping man and bends down near his tired, frowning face. I am sure she is about to commit an act of violence or psychosis or both and so I hesitate and pause. But she bends down and softly, as though her fingers were made of silk, removes the man's glasses from his eyes, folds them and places them near his head so he will find them when he wakes. I feel ashamed; this possibility of care never occurred to me.

The second happens nearby, in the early twilight, while I am out walking my dogs. I see two ambulances, parked one in front of another, the doors of the first are open and from where I stand, I see a stretcher, pale legs, a cracked sole and another foot in a bandage. It doesn't seem to be a serious accident but still I walk carefully, not wanting to see something terrible. But the dogs are dawdling so I have to dawdle with them and without wanting to I see the injured person, a woman I think, from the hands. I can't hear her, but I see that she is in distress, waving her arms at the paramedics. They crowd around her, masks hanging variously under and over their noses, trying to communicate with their patient. The woman grows more agitated (the dogs, calmer, one sniffing a leaf then a tree trunk, another licking the pavement) her thin hands grasping, flailing in the air. She is panicked, growing more frantic until something happens: she makes contact with one of the paramedics. Her hands grab onto the paramedic's arms and they calm, she calms. I see her run her hands along the paramedic's forearms, tenderly. Her whole body stills then, soothed, her hands holding and touching a stranger with something I can only describe as communion. The scene seems to slow down, arrested by the very magic of touch. Whatever she has been searching for, she has found. She's no longer afraid.

The third is less dramatic. I hear a neighbour I am quite sure I hate, singing. His voice, for the briefest of moments, is beautiful and I forget my animosity.

Poetry is the art of the ordinary, the invisible, and the everyday. It is the true art of the people. In its ability to reach out and connect us to the tremors and longings of the world around us, it reminds us constantly about the power to surprise. As the chair judge of the Forward Prizes, to spend the better part of a year thinking about poetry has been an incredible gift. The collections we pored over reminded me of care and the power strangers exert over each other in so many delicate and fragile ways. The poets we read and selected have, to paraphrase Frank O'Hara, investigated the laws of their own voices but also contemporary society, queerness, politics, feminism, friendship, loneliness and more.

We have assembled here a collection of debut writers, masters, believers and doubters, all of them innate observers of our intimate lives. Some of them you may already know, others will be a revelation. Whether they are writing about grief, joy, migration, war, or modern life, they allow their readers a certain kind of rebirth: stopping and lifting us from the chaos of whatever we are doing and redirecting our attention to something urgent, perhaps even something beautiful. Attention, Simone Weil wrote, is a form of prayer. And in returning our attention to us, poetry redeems us. It returns us to our natural state, one of wonder. Though all these poems are animated by a quiet force, one of conviction, there is no singularity to them. They are questioning, funny, profound and all of them glorious.

Fatima Bhutto
Chair of Judges
June 2022

Preface

Anniversaries have been very much on my mind on this, the 30th anniversary of the Prizes. The Best First Collection prize was *first* awarded in 1992 to our current Poet Laureate Simon Armitage for his extraordinary collection, *Kid*. He was joined onstage by Thom Gunn, who received Best Collection that year, and Jackie Kay, who won Best Single Poem.

I founded Forward all those years ago because I thought it was important to showcase the best new poetry, and to try to build bigger, more diverse audiences for poetry – to bring poetry out of poetry corner. Our aim was to focus on the *new*, the contemporary, the lived experience of the present we collectively occupy, and 30 years later, that's still very much at the heart of what we do. We seek out the new, and we hope to offer a range of voices, both new and old, emerging and established. But eventually the new become established, the emerging always emerging. This is the nature of new, it will one day also evolve into something that must been marked and commemorated.

And poetry has always been the artform we turn to most frequently to commemorate and mark, to remember and reflect. It is the ideal artform for an anniversary – and unprecedented times. The best new writing engages with both the past and a present. It is very much rooted in a moment, but also continues to speak to us long beyond that fleeting thing.

The present volume is very much a testament to this duality. It is both a vessel to give witness to the last two years, but also engages in a much wider conversation across time and place. Most of all, this volume is an attempt at connecting across time and space: Every poet here is in conversation with a multitude of poets that have come before: in their brilliant Q&As, they flag Sappho, Rabia, Mahadeviyakaa, Walcott and Ginsburg, Sharon Olds and Carolyn Forche, Vahni Anthony Ezekiel Capildeo and Natalie Diaz, and even each other as inspiration. They are also in conversation with each other, and *with you*, the reader.

This year's judges read 217 full collections and 192 single poems; to arrive at a shortlist of 5 in each category was a daunting task for our esteemed judges, and in their meetings, the word 'responsibility' recurred: this was not a task they took lightly. As fellow creatives (novelist, poets, performers), they knew what effort went into the work behind every line, *every* word, and they felt the enormity of what each poet does in sending this work out into the world.

It brought home to all of us at Forward that our mission is not one we take lightly: It's a gift that we're still here 30 years on, with the enviable task of highlighting the incredible strength and vitality of poetry in the UK today through the awards and the present volume.

None of this – of course – would be possible without the dedication of our five judges this year: novelist and activist Fatima Bhutto and poets Rishi Dastidar, alice hiller, Nadine Aisha Jassat, and Stephen Sexton. They received box after box of submissions with good humour, care and consideration. We are deeply inspired in their approach to these Prizes.

We are grateful to our funders: Bookmark Content, which has supported us from the very beginning; the Arts Council England; the Charlotte Aitken Trust, which has supported the production and printing of this book; the Felix Dennis Estate, which supports the Best First Collection Prize; the Garfield Weston Foundation and a number of individual donors. Thank you, too, to fellow Trustees of the Forward Arts Foundation: Jamie Andrews, Mary Amanuel, Kim Evans, Aoife O'Connor, Maya Ophelia, Amelia Richards and Giles Spackman. And thank you to our outgoing chair, Martin Thomas, for 8 years of service.

Thank you to the Forward Arts Foundation team – Jay Bhadricha, Omar Fadhil, Lucy Macnab and Mónica Parle – who have navigated a lot of change across the pandemic. This is an entirely new team and they have set to work on creating a new vision and future strategy to see us into the next 30 years.

William Sieghart
Founder of the Forward Prizes for Poetry
June 2022

The Forward Book of Poetry

2023

Shortlisted Poems
The Forward Prize for Best Collection

Kaveh Akbar

Reza's Restaurant, Chicago, 1997

the waiters milled about filling sumac
                 shakers clearing away
plates of onion and radish
my father pointed to each person whispered
Persian about the old man with the silver
                 beard whispered *Arab* about the woman with
   the eye mole *Persian* the teenager pouring
water *White* the man on the phone
                                    I was eight
              still soft as a thumb and amazed
I asked how he could possibly tell when
                                    they were all brown-
skin-dark-haired like us almost everyone
              in the restaurant looked like us
                       he smiled a proud
              little smile a warm nest
of lip said *it's easy* said *we're just uglier*

                 he returned to his lamb but I was baffled hardly
touched my gheimeh I had big glasses and bad
          teeth I felt plenty Persian
                                    when the woman
          with light eyes and blonde-brown
hair left our check my father looked at me
          I said *Arab?* he shook his head laughed
              we drove home I grew up it took years to
          put together what my father
meant that day my father who listened
          exclusively to the Rolling Stones
who called the Beatles
              a band for girls
          my father who wore only black even
              around the house whose umbrella

5

made it rain whose arms could
          cut chicken wire and make stew and
   bulged with old farm scars my father my
father my father built
   the world the first sound I ever heard
       was his voice whispering the azan
         in my right ear I didn't need anything
        else my father cherished
      that we were ugly and so being ugly
          was blessed I smiled with all my teeth

Reading Farrokhzad in a Pandemic

The title is a lie;
I can't read Farsi.

ما هر چه را که باید از دست داده باشیم از دست داده ایم

I can make out:

'we lose,
we lose.'

I type it into a translation app:
'we have lost everything we need to lose.'

In between what I read and what is written:
'need,' 'everything.'

　　　　□

Here, the waving flag.
Here, the other world.

Because we need mail, people die.

　　　　□

Because we need groceries, people die.

I write '*we* need'
knowing *we* dilutes

　　　　□

my responsibility,
like watercolors dipped

in a fast river.
Get behind me, English.

□

When I text
ما هر چه را که باید از دست داده باشیم از دست داده ایم

to my dad he writes back,
'we have lost whatever we had to lose.'

Hammering
pentameter.

Whatever we
had.

People die because they look like him.
My uncle jailed, his daughter killed.

□

This a real fact too wretched for
letters. And yet:

My uncle jailed.

□

His daughter killed.

Waving world,
the other flag—

there is room in the language for being
without language.

□

So much of *wet* is *cold*.
So much of *diamond* is *light*.

□

I want both my countries
to be right

to fear me.

We have lost
whatever

we had to lose.

Anthony Joseph

Jogie Road

From life, from love, in shame. The red
sawmill on Jogie Road with cedar grain
in its fibrous air. Red. The old train
track and the bridge where my mother's rage
was bruising the dark. Her fingernails ripped
at my father's shirt, his face.
This is blood: the way he looks away,
then down with open palms in resignation.
But memory has a curious sting. The red sawmill
was not on Jogie Road but on Silvermill.
And in the savannah there were five saman trees
which cried when cut, not six.
My father held me over his shoulder that night.
No, I was looking up from the road.

Trinidad, 17 November 1970

Breath

When I hear my father dead,
I flew ten hours into the sun.
Next morning, I put black on.
Waistcoat, white shirt, soft pants,
the new brown half-brogues.

The deep brakes of the rental car
were unsuitable for islands.
Every time I fall asleep I driving off the road.
And when that casket was flung open in the chapel
I was not prepared for what I saw.

Outside, the sun continued lancing the galvanise,
and the San Juan River to run towards the south.
There was no wind, no breath in that hot time,
besides the warm air above my father's mouth.

Shane McCrae

The Butterflies the Mountain and the Lake

It's Saturday   most often neighbor   we
Are walking with our daughter lately   even when / We walk together
everywhere we go we want to go home everywhere   / But oh
hey did you see that story

about the butterflies the mountain and the lake
the   / Butterflies monarch butterflies huge swarms they
Migrate and as they migrate south   as they
Cross Lake Superior instead of flying

South straight across they fly
South over the water then fly east
still over the water then fly south   again / And now
biologists believe they   turn to avoid a mountain

That disappeared millennia ago   / No
butterfly lives long enough to fly   the whole migration
From the beginning to the end
they / Lay eggs along the way

Just as you and I   most often neighbor
Migrate together in our daughter   over a dark lake
We make with joy the child we make
And mountains are reborn in her

Eurydice on the Art of Poetry

The story you have   heard is false   it's true
He sang for me   and true he lulled the god
Who didn't care to fight him   easily
The god is like us all   the blood of the dead

Is made wine by their sorrow some   don't argue
And others never stop   I followed him
Yes but he wasn't   told he couldn't look
He didn't look because he felt ashamed

I know now he already had the poem
Finished or nearly   so before he left
For the underworld   he didn't come for me
He came to check the details   he had thought

He'd fail to win me back   and in the end
Yes   at the mouth of the cave he just ran off
I think he didn't know what else to do
I didn't follow him   it was a relief

To be allowed to keep my death   I heard
The poem first in the spring   sung by a new-
ly murdered boy who didn't know my name
When he was told my name   why should he have

I wasn't in the poem   the poem was true

Kim Moore

16.

When you rewind what happened, your fist
moving away from my face, your arm pulling back,
tracing a half moon in the air, do you watch yourself
running backwards from the flat,
that moment and all of its violence unfrozen,
do you imagine me rising from the bed,
the look on my face before I answer the door?
Do your words return and push themselves back
into your mouth, are you forced to swallow them
again and again? Not *sorry* but *you fucking bitch*,
those words and ones like them, finally lifting from my skin.

I know the living can haunt the living without trying.
Slag. Slut. If I imagine our lives in reverse,
my eyes are always lifting from the floor,
good things are happening. Are you watching
as I vanish into the last gasp of a bus,
reversing through the city? Sometimes I imagine
seeing you again, back row of chairs at an event,
your arms folded, listening to me read
about transformation and violence and loss.
You cannot touch me when I'm speaking,
though what I'm speaking about is us.

42.

Is it ▮ if your husband/boyfriend/friend did it, is it ▮ if you didn't say no/yes, if you were arguing/not speaking, is it ▮ if he spits in your face and you just want it to stop, is it ▮ if you can't even write it, is it ▮ if you can't even say it, if you opened your legs, if you didn't protest, if you stayed with him after, is it ▮ if you pretend nothing has happened, is it ▮ if you did it to distract him, to make him stop shouting, to make him stop swearing, to make him stop leaving, is it ▮ if you became grey, if some bright fish of desire went into hiding for years, is it ▮ if you were frightened, not for your life, but for your mind, is it ▮ if your mind was slipping away and doing it was the only thing that stopped the slipping, is it ▮ if you did it so you could sleep, is it ▮ if you did it to stand in for forgiveness, if you had hate in your heart when you did it, if you had lies in your chest, is it ▮ if you didn't mean it, if you can't remember what happened, is it still ▮ if you never told anyone, if you didn't think about it again, if you moved on, if you're ok now, if you're ok now, if you're ok now.

Helen Mort

A Well-known Beach

This study examined the approach behaviour of men
to women lying on a well-known beach.

The women were reading, (well-known)
lying flat on their stomachs

some with a tattoo prominently displayed
on their lower backs. On a well-known beach,

women were reading, (flat
on their well-known stomachs)

some with a tattoo on their lower backs,
some without. On a well-known beach

men were more likely to approach
the women with visible tattoos

not because they found them
to be more attractive but because

the women (well-known reading
on their lower backs) because

they believed the tattooed women
(the men well-known, the women lying

on their flat stomachs)
but because they believed the tattooed women

would be more likely to have sex
(well-known prominently displayed

on their lower backs)
more likely to have sex

on the first date
than their clear-skinned counterparts.

Source: Psychology Today: What People Really Think About Women With Tattoos

Loch Allua

'*Every swim is a little death*' – PHILIP HOARE

Your body yellow
when you glance back –
a naked flame, trapped
beneath the brown glass

but – yes – you move,
you almost flicker, kicking
out towards the deepest part,
blood in your wrists ticking.

Where will you go now?
You who have never known
which shore to swim for
or which rock to call your own.

Ahead of you,
the coarse hair of the trees,
the bog beyond,
the path towards the sea.

Behind you, sunlight
and the knuckled limestone,
ground brindled with moss,
the crickets' single tone.

And God, how easy
it would be to let your arms
go slack and let the water
veil your face, lean back

and into it, your mouth
slow-opening like a fish.
But even as you almost
grant yourself the wish,

you know you are at heart
a woman who must swim.
Above your head,
three swallows dive and skim

in navy uniforms,
unbuttoned from the sky.
Watch this. How close they swoop
before they're lifted high.

Shortlisted Poems
The Felix Dennis Prize for Best First Collection

Mohammed El-Kurd

Boy Sells Gum at Qalandiyah

The question is not morality, the question is money.
That's what we're upset about.
                              – Toni Morrison

There are bulldozers in these clouds. Bulldozers
in their clouds and they bring rain often. A boy
at Qalandiyah and they have stolen the wicks of
the stars. He shouldn't be outside. Stones will fling
themselves in protest.

This Hebrewed land still speaks Arabic. Their
drones will rig this. The boy at Qalandiyah selling
gum. He shouldn't be outside. He'll be a thrower, a
catcher. A bulldozed bulldozer. Often.

What's a boy doing winning bread under gallows?
And where's the merit in that? Whose side is God
on? Some days it feels like they've unlocked prayer.
They prey often.

A man on the sidewalk explains natural selection.
As in the boy's grip shouldn't be softened. The man
says the boy's walk looks too much like a song and
too little like a man walking.

A woman tells him a pen is a sword. What's a pen
to a rifle? Another fed him a sonnet. If Shakespeare
was from here he wouldn't be writing.

I write about Palestinian boys as if they're older
than labor.

The boy is eight, which is twenty-two for Americans. The boy knows this. His mother calls him a man in his nightmares. *You're a man now.* A painter stands in this, collecting strokes. A photographer offers a helping hand. They want to build a museum in his torture. The boy wins the bread knowing he shouldn't be.

He tells the photographer to pay him for his bread; the photographer's bread. For wallets fattened by indigence.

His mother calls him the man of the house. She thinks it makes him feel better about the hunched back he's earned before the 6 a.m. of his life. The gray he's earned before the 6 a.m. of his life. Qalandiyah is gray often.

I drive by. I roll down my window. I buy what I can. *You shouldn't be outside through the fire.* What is fear to the ferocious? I ask him to stop selling gum. He tells me I don't know a thing about this. Don't know a thing about the sun's fingernails clawing the back of his neck.
I'll be quiet then.
I don't know a thing,   truly,
Not a man   yet.   Not a man   often.

Bulldozers Undoing God

for Mahfoutha Ishtayyeh

A chain is corseting
the tree's waist and hers,
flesh in flesh,
      olive skin on olive skin,
fingers   branches   intersections
      rootedness jars their storms,
               wraps them
in her unbreakable word
          we will not leave.
              Leave!

She clings onto the tree trunk
      the feeling afore the drown.

Land   stone and dirt, pillowed
      buried ones and ones lying
      contaminated reality
      numbed faith, indulged upon
      embroidered destinies
      constant Nakbas
      tragedy pillowed and bedroomed
made normal: mornings of mourning
on a breakfast table,
      olives
      za'atar
      tomatoes and cucumber
      tragedy
      tear gas and tea

In Jerusalem, every footstep is a grave.

This was only love:
her skeleton is that of the tree's,
roots stitched into land into identity.
Separation is like

> unmaking love
> ungluing names to places
> undoing God.

> A pulling pressure, soldiered:
> occupiers occupy her limbs,
> untangling a grandmother.
> A soldier as old as a leaf born yesterday
> pulls a trigger on a woman older than his heritage.

> Two martyrs fall.

> One
> martyr
> falls.

> Here, every footstep is a grave,
> every grandmother is a Jerusalem.

Holly Hopkins

Telephone Girls

Girls have always been joined to telephone systems.
Not just teenage gossips or nineteen-forties girls
in whale-fat lipstick, scalps smelling
of chemical burns for days after each perm,
girls plugged into circuit boards, primed for scandal,
heavy bakelite ear cones and mouthpieces rising
like snakes' heads up from their breasts;
that's not what I mean.
I mean anchorites – telephones to God.

They chose to be built into church walls:
Dame Julian of Norwich,
Emma of All Saints, North Street, York;
the masonry rising like a slow upward guillotine.
The simple engineers would leave a slot
to admit a parcel of light and air,
food and requested prayers.

They believed that in this pure removal
they'd become a prayer machine.
That each day of silence would be another stitch
sewing their lips and ears into the robes of God,
until their tears would fall directly in his lap.

Explanation for Those Who Don't Know Love

I have a child and am more important
than childless people.

I am two people and have an extra vote.
You cannot comprehend our bond,

it is mysterious and I am greater because of it,
so in a tie-break situation I am three people.

My daughter is five and very bright for her age,
this requires special consideration.

She is a delight and centres every conversation
like a fantastic table decoration.

If she breaks your possessions
it's an interrogation of their meaning,

a state of blissful questioning you have lost.
If she cries it's only because she wants something.

She can't yet comprehend the magnitude of grief
so it is not selfish like when you cry.

Padraig Regan

50ml of India Ink

Opaque, & black as gravity,
the ink is perfectly unlike

the small glass pot
whose shape it occupies

so passively. It is
something's burnt remains

that makes it black.
It is the sticky leavings

of the lac-bug
that makes it shine.

(The name of the lac-bug
has nothing to do

with absence, but means,
in fact, a multitude.)

It performs its tiny fractal
creep through the paper's

knitted capillaries,
& finds itself astounded

with significance. It means
I am not yet dead.

I was not untempted
to leave this blank.

Salt Island

I wanted to make a gothic of it all:
the trees on the slope where the island dipped
            into the sea, their weird kinks & angles;
the scrap of wool where a sheep had rubbed
            a flank against a tree's arthritic fingers;
the cloud-quilt which was then breaking up
            as though someone had pulled
the one thread which held the whole clump
            of vapours in place. I walked over
the hill with my kilt flapping
                                & thought
            wow! all this for me? &
the weather just kept getting better,
            rescinding its earlier threats of rain.
The mood was ruined; I wanted ice-cream.
            In the photographs I scroll through now,
in bed a week later, I see that my red tartan
            clashed with the grass so perfectly
I wonder if I intended to be the punctum,
            the little rip in the surface
where my eye might snag. It is too
            early to tell if I've succeeded,
& too early in the morning — the sun
            not yet visible behind the hills —
to tease out what it means when all this naming,
            of the island, wool, sheep, trees, & clouds,
is just another way of saying I, I, I, I, I

Warsan Shire

Bless Grace Jones

Holy Mother of those deemed intimidating,
patron saint of the unapproachable,
saviour of those told to soften their expression.

Our lady of uncomfortable silences,
Dame Grace Jones, your daughters
(damn their insomnia) turn in their dreamless sleep,
a legion of women flinching at touch.
Fortify them.

Monarch of the last word,
darling of the dark, arched brow,
we bless you, queen of the cut eye.

We lay our burdens at your feet,
careful not to weigh you down,
                    from you, we are learning
to put ourselves first.

Midnight in the Foreign Food Aisle

Dear Uncle, is everything you love foreign
or are you foreign to everything you love?
We're all animals and the body wants what
it wants, trust me, I know. The blonde said
*Come in, love, take off your coat, what do
you want to drink?*

Love is not haram but after years of fucking
women who are unable to pronounce your name,
you find yourself totally alone, in the foreign
food aisle, beside the turmeric and saffron,
remembering your mother's warm, dark hands,
prostrating in front of the halal meat, praying in a
language you haven't used in years.

Stephanie Sy-Quia

extracts from *Amnion*

Of Canterbury I recall
scuff
stone smell
shoe seep
smell at crotch of tights
'blazer'.

To the school: I am delivered. A three-hour drive north, through a valed
land replete with cathedrals. There is Amiens, with its traces of paint, still;
and Chartres of the windows; Beauvais, unfinished – three times its spire
fell through; now it is braced with wooden beams: on crutches. It boasts
the highest clerestory in Europe, it smells of mouldering stone. Rheims
where are buried the kings; Coulombs which boasts the foreskin of the
Saviour. Under the Channel, to burst forth near a hill where runs a horse
white in chalk.

(I remember that boat, smallest to answer the call.)
(Named Tamzine, it lies on the floor of the museum for imperial war.)
(The littlest of the little ships of Dunkirk,
clinker-built from Canadian spruce.)

The school is of flint and brick, it too has a cathedral.

At the boarding house, which is new, but built out of the ruins of the old
infirmary ten centuries old, another mother is wearing a poncho. She asks
where we're from, how we got here. At my mother's reply (the Eurotunnel)
she says *Oh well you will have come in under our land then.*

I am unpacked and stowed away.

Later that night, the others start to arrive. There are five blondes in a total
of twelve. There is lacrosse gear and lurid pink mouthguards. Their jeans
are different from mine (tighter). I have never seen so many sets of big
breasts. Their hair is mid-length (it swishes). Their clothes are all
somehow the same.

– Are you rich?

(The others wait politely for my reply)

The land seemed so old, but deluded also.
The white horse that leaps on the green hill, singing in chalk,
is a copy.
The stone of the cathedral came from Caen, where as a child in an
oversized fleece
I stood in a very large crater near the Museum of Peace.
'My father was at D-Day and was shot in the hip, he lay on the beach in
the surf for three days.'
My godfather has my baby sister strapped to his chest.
This cool cold plain of Europe's beige edge is on par with Mont St Michel,
its
great flat-footed expanse where my brother and I dig its ridges for clams
before the tide
comes running.
This is deep bone-knowing country.

Albion.

I hold it in my mouth with pleasure like a corp
ulent pearl.
It contains all the stories England tells itself:
a plosive, bounded space, girded by neat cliffs and land's end.
How they thought of their virgin queen,
the whole universe under her skirts.

The dean beckoned me and with his thumb
Upon my forehead said *admitto te*
And I having for sole reference the Simba smudge, stumbled on the stiff
white surplice lent to me on a two-year lease.

They were so blithe about the signifiers of their station. They had hairless
pits and thighs, and paid, from the age of not yet fucking or fingering, for
bikini waxes. They had an easy greed and met me with incomprehension
when I tried in vain to explain where I came from.

Food was a thing ingested under mild duress.

My femalehood was boarded over my eyes like a set piece.
To determine its deviance became the all-consuming aim.
Cover your shoulders.
Shoulders remind boys of boobs.
My body became as incendiary as a vernacular.
It was the thing that lay in the dark woods at the trailing ends of
sentences,
at the short edge of night and late at skirt.

The blonde others aspired to be described with mean, hard-nosed little
words: thin, pretty, nice.
I wanted big-femur words like wise and kind.

The boys were always
touching
each other.

When the parents came, they were loud.
They came two by two in pairs of Sunday-lunching racists.
The fathers wore trousers the colour of rare meat.

(A hunk of roast beef seeping)
(banking on things in the city)
(with flats, useful for unfaithing.)
Their wives stayed at home, in the counties. Maybe they were lonely, and screamed
themselves hoarse in the cut-stone quiet of their houses.
These marriages seemed structures of mutual scorn.
Watching them made me flush hot with fear that this was coming for me
and sent me knock-kneed to hide.
Their days of Barbour-ed torpor; the cream-coloured afternoons –

I wanted big-beamed love. I wanted to be one of the women who swear
and have grey in their hair. I wanted, though this too was warped, to be
the emotional centre without which nothing can hold.

In our lesson the time-lined people have made landfall in America. The
people they find there are untime-lined, according to the landfalls they
have no history. This is something that even the ancients did not know.
This is something entirely new. Everything is uncertain. The world is of
unknown proportions. Luther is nailing a piece of paper to a door. He is
standing saying I stand before you now and can do no other. Everything is
chaos. Nothing is known. The universe is a black womb rioting with stars.

On the staircase in the history block was a framed print
         WE SHALL FIGHT THEM ON THE BEACHES
all around it dotted coats of arms and rays of light, which seemed a slight
confusion.

I AM WRITING NOW from the inky heart of empire,
its assonance no more unknown to me.
I shall knock the pillars out from under you
and label you up
in room upon room
of Wedgwood blue.

I HAVE SHUFFLED ALL THE SHARDS of what came to me broken
and I have not pried, for dealing in shards is what I wanted;
these being my inheritance.

THESE BEING
my demands
my thanks
my by rights

I USED TO WORRY that the performance was never quite for my own
benefit;
that I owed it to others, that without me they might never apprehend and
therefore I was duty-bound to make the point
again and again,
with the quiet militancy of washing rice before cooking it in a saucepan.
This had been the extent of it: cooking rice.
But it is possible, as I have found, to delineate blood-bearings to each
their own.
My brother, for instance, is less interested in this quandary.
My father, for instance, professes to be half, which would make me a
quarter.
I reserve his right to do so; but my claim is my own.
                              (And when it comes to the men of my family,
                                   I do not think it has nothing to do with
                                        their command of desire, depending.)

Who was Emaré?
One who was given a coat embroidered with love stories
so that when donned
she was clothed in romance.

She fled.
She wandered.
The coat weighed.
Until she cast it off.
And then,
she was free.
Her shoulders bare
with their allusive curves.

All the uses of my body and what others would have me put it to.
Blood is so contrived.
Texts are porous.
I am walking
from one
to the other.
I am clothed in romance.
I am casting it off.

Like this I am primeval as a woman in a sundress.
I have become one of the gritty women, with freckles peppering the loose
skin of their arms.
I am walking through a many-furrowed field
which in relinquished seasons is feathered with asparagus.
In this late light of an early century, the ash shades of earth and stubble,
I plight (give, pledge) you my troth (fealty, loyalty, truth).

Palazzo della Signoria – the ceiling with Penelope and other female
virtues (on business with my mother. In the evenings, mozzarella that
oozed with the pleasure of being eaten). Even then, I had inklings: when I
looked at the female virtues on the ceiling.

(The position I would need to be in to contemplate
Esther sitting strong in her faith.)

And when the stories are shrugged from my shoulders, then I am free.
You are the bedrock of all that I am.
All the days of my life
shall be to honour you
in every thing I do.
Now I walk.

A marriage should not be a forsaking of all others. It is instead a many-
witnessed act. I stand before you today (I imagine myself saying) with the
emotional health to choose this person because of all of you. I can face the
enormity of this decision because of you. I know what love is because of
you: its bluntness, its grittiness.

I am here, the bottom bracket of a most-loathed generation.
All the joys promised to me. And those potencies playing out in other
theatres of war,
our little civilian lives of hitherto peace
the future endless no more,
violence, like money, stored offshore.
Your coming over the threshold was marked.
My equivalent days were opposed.
It was stark.
When we came over the hill with our knuckles all in our mouths,
it was something I'd seen:
a hit-and-run future which had come for us like the slice of a knife.
And the world we knew was all wrong: too hot, and unjust.

Nonetheless, your coming was heralded with the triumphs of the civilian
over regime.
Let us enter into oaths knowingly. So I ask you now in the presence of this
company.

> ('And of course,' volunteered my father
> to my friend, 'my best friend, I married.')

In defiance of state.

It is the vowing which interests me.
I call upon these persons here present.
The cause for which marriage was ordained (this is not included in the
civil script, having been cut in twain at the time of the burnings)
to love and to cherish
from this day forward
incumbent on me
all that I am I give to you.

> (but were they their all, at the time of
> their giving? And how did they know?)
> (I am suspicious of this knowledge which apparently simply descends.)

Then they shall give their troth to each other.

> (the deep bone know)

from this day forward
put asunder
against all manner of foes.
Have you never been held by all the limbs of a woman?

Callum and I eat a cheese. We walk for hours and look at art.
Arthur makes a single Yorkshire pudding which looks like Anatolia.
I am making little waves with my carrot, as if it were a cigarette.

There are long conversations: in bars, in kitchens, in the illegal extensions of council house flats. We get drunk too much. We know nothing about wine. We spend our money on shoes. We press our palms together to dance in the amber-coloured oak-panelled dark. We bowl forth to a city that didn't really want us.

Would I live forever in this country?
The thought made my throat close in.
Its chalky mid-hues. Fields like paint sample cards with whimsical names.
I will love you all my life.

When my mother vowed in the face of those persons then present
to commit to my father to the exclusion of all others,
that cold day in October with the Assyrian lions
and the red buses streaking by,
the imminent grapes,
my mother was protecting my father from the violence which could come
for him
in the night or the day, at work or at rest,
and take him back to the islands where little love waited for him.
My mother was twenty-one, bullish and
knew nothing.
It was her boldest act in the time of walls falling.

All over the world.
My father resents this narrative.
He says it was love.
Which it was.
But we must not forget
the bodies that eyed this union for a full year after.
My parents are brave
and the choices I make will be made
in the vault of this precedent.

Shortlisted Poems
The Forward Prize for Best Single Poem

Louisa Campbell

Dog on a British Airways Airbus 319–100

human human human human human human
human human human human human human
human human human human human human
human human human human human human
human human human human human human
human human human human human human
human human human human human human
human human human human human human
human human human human human human
human human human human human human
human human human human human human
human human human human human human
human human human human human human
human human human human human human
human dog human human human human
human human human human human human
human human human human human human
human human human human human human
human human human human human human
human human human human human human
human human human human human human
human human human
human human

Cecilia Knapp

I'm Shouting I LOVED YOUR DAD at my Brother's Cat

I'm crying at green wallpaper
sick with the memory of your hands.
When you died, though I'd asked you not to,
I got some rest. Fair play. I ate my eggs
and the sun came out. How do you enjoy a fuck
when you're sunburnt with grief?
I had hoped for a loss of appetite,
some silver lining. I live in a flat
that I can't afford. It's got big windows.
They get so dirty. I don't condition my hair.
You'd be disappointed at how often
I let myself go.
I've got your name tattooed on my finger,
but it keeps falling off
when I do the washing up.
I've kept that cat you poured your tenderness into.
I don't remember kissing you
but that doesn't mean it didn't happen.
Some days it's someone else's brother.
You serve me in a coffee shop.
You're on the mend,
pierced ears and a soft hat.

Nick Laird

Up Late

If I shut my eyes to the new dark
I find that I start to experience time
in its purest state: a series of durations
rising and dilating beneath my inwards gaze:
an eruptive core where the umbra blooms
in crestless waves of darkness as within
another umbra bubbles up from the interior –
from nothingness, from nowhere –
and at the centre of the crest of this
disintegrating, reassembling nest
the jet of time generates, is consciousness,
the planetary mind, aloft, alone, mine,
jostled and spun like a ping pong ball.

*

My father died today. Sorry to bolt that on.
You understand the shift required. This morning
the consultant said your father now is clawing
at the mask and is exhausted and we've thrown
everything we have at this. It's a terrible disease.

He promises to give him morphine and that a nurse
will be beside him at all times to hold his hand
and talk him through it.
It being the transition,
the change of state, the fall of light, the trade,

the instant of the hand itself turning from the subject
into object. No, we are not allowed in the ward
and there cannot be exceptions. Thank you for making
this difficult call. But I know what the body wants.
Continuance. Continuance. Continuance
at any cost.

*

But dying, then, as we speak,
my father in the IC ward
of Antrim Area Hospital.

The icy ward.
The ICU.
I see you too.

On Sunday they permitted us to Zoom
and he was prone in a hospital gown

strapped to a white slab.
The hospital gown split at the back
and the pale cold skin of his back was exposed.

He lifted his head to the camera
and his face was all red, swollen,
bisected vertically by the mask,
and we had to ask Elizabeth the nurse
to say his words back to us –
he sounded underwater –
it's been a busy day but not a good day.

*

I could see even with the mask on
your little satisfaction with the phrase
managed out.

And the achievement left you
so depleted you lowered your head
back to the slab, having done with us,

like some seal on a rock looking up
as we pass on the Blue Pool ferry
out to Garinish.
                    Dad,
you poor bastard, I see you.

You lay like that for a week alone
with your thoughts in the room.

Tethered. Breathless. Undefended.
At sea as on an ice floe
slipping down into the shipping channels.

*

The eye adjusts, even to darkness,
even to the presence of what overwhelms us,
and as I make my way from the bed to the study
the soles of my feet on the carpet warp it
as any fabric made of this space-time will distort
beneath the force of a large object – and my father,
as it happens, is gigantic – and if you thought
an understanding could be reached, you are wrong
for it could not.
                    The goldfish pilots the light of itself
through a ten-gallon darkness and I keep watch
as the large hand of the clock covers the small
and leaves it behind to the weak approximation
I sit here in and finish writing.

*

I want the poem to destroy time.
What are the ceremonies of forgetting?

There is a spring in Boetia
that lets the river Lethe enter the world.

King Gjuki's ale of forgetfulness.
Excessive phlegm.

But I like the notion of the angel
lightly tapping the baby

in its soft hollow above the top lip, erasing
all the child knows,

all its regret, all its terrible grief,
before it descends again fresh to the world.

*

After your stroke you were born once more
as smaller, greyer, softer, and after Mum died,
left bewildered, adrift, ordering crap online
and following the auctions, the horses, the football,
the golf – but hungering for company, for anyone,

sending money to that Kenyan who was younger
than me and flying out to Germany to see her,
and again, before Jackie arrived on the scene,
the divorced blonde who had 'her demons',
by which you meant she was a violent alcoholic,
though with Louise things seemed steady enough,
for a few months, before you got stuck in one
of your loops about her ex-husband funding her
and the weird behavior of her ingrate daughter.

*

You could never let anything go, a trait
I also suffer from, and kind of admire, but

this is not a possibility. The tick of the clock
is meltwater dripping into the fissure.

The minute hand clicks across the hour hand
and hovers for a minute, exactly,

and impinging on the vision is your slack wild face
and the way a nurse's hand might hold

your cold hand or try again to lift your hand
but your hand now will not respond.

*

I have been writing elegies for you all my life, Father,
in one form or another, but now I find the path is just
this game trail through the forest, the forested mind
and I would follow in the manner of an animal –
a deer, a fox, a chimpanzee – returning to the clearing
to nuzzle the corpse, to lick its nape or bite it softly,
to look away, and look again, and wait for a response.
One hand on the clock holds the other for a minute
before going on alone. It is death that is implicit
in the ticking.

*

One must negotiate the next moment. The mind
will not stop and certain things are good to think
with. Goldfish; carpet; clock. I want something fit
to mediate the procreative business of redoubling
the brittle world, and settle on an image, for a second,
since it is a given that the mind will keep returning
to the magic, the legerdemain, the trick: one hand
holding your hand as it turns into an object, as I turn
back along the track toward the fold, toward
the corner of the field where the father's body lies,
and with an animal's dumb clarity do grief work –
kiss your hand and kiss your cheek and leave
my forehead for a time pressed against yours.

*

When I phoned the hospital this afternoon
to say goodbye, though you were no longer lucid,

Elizabeth the nurse held the phone against your ear
and I could hear your breathing, or perhaps the rasping

of the oxygen machine, and I said what you'd expect.
I love you, Dad, and I want you to keep on fighting,

but if you are too tired now, and in too much pain,
then you should stop fighting, and let go, and whatever

happens it's okay. I love you. You were a good father.
The kids love you. Thank you for everything.

Then I hung up. And scene. Impossible to grieve
and not know the vanity of grief. To watch one

self perform the rituals that take us. Automaton
of grief, I howled, of course, by myself

in my office, then sobbed for a bit on the sofa.
An elegy I think is words to bind a grief

in, a companionship of grief, a spell
to keep it safe and sound, to keep it

from escaping. There are various ways to
memorize. Plato calls on Mnemosyne.

My grandfather Bertie liked to tie
a knot in his blue handkerchief.

My father wrote in biro on his palm.
I cannot leave the poem alone.

*

Do you remember the pure world? I remember it
from being a kid. All was at stake in that place,
one moved through it sideways, through forests
of time, lost in them, and had to be called back
to the moment. Infinities growing in stone,
in moss, in the hayshed, the rain, the wind,
in the darkness under the cattle grid.

Rilke says of the pure unseparated element –
'. . . someone dies and *is* it.'

*

It's after two.
You are dead by now I hope.
Who thought to write that?

There's no hurry now,
no effort, no need to call.
You might be only sitting

in your red chair
endlessly flicking
through the channels.

*

When I asked the doctor, Andrew Black, he said,
it could take minutes, it could take hours,

and I see you slumped, not sitting up,
propped against some pillows

with your eyes closed. Something in you
finally given up defying gravity,

some obedience to objecthood settled
in you now and set up home. Set in stone.

Outside on the motorway the headlights
of the vehicles are necklaces of diamonds,

double-strung, and alongside them,
heading westwards, necklaces of garnets.
                                        Dad,
I cannot stay in the room with you too
long in my mind. It is too hard. I thought

there would be futurity. I thought things
would happen. Nothing major. Barbecues.

Why barbecues? God knows. You are walking
round Bantry at the Friday market in your shorts

in the rain, your white tube socks pulled tightly up
and a bright t-shirt from some Spanish golf trip

tucked into your shorts. By the way,
we are even, you and I. No need. Look:

How absolutely still the room is. Outside
the widowed sky has grown huge with stars.

The Milky Way meandering like the Ballinderry,
though the night has come with work to do.

It sits with you and broods. It wants you
to come at your own pace. And at this moment

you might get up and speak clearly to everything,
creation, extinction, infinities rising within you.

*

Alastair Laird is dead. Fuckety fuck. Fuckety
fuck fuck fuck fuck. My dad is dead. Bad luck.
The light breaks and the night breaks and the line
breaks and the day is late assembling. Rows
of terraced houses are clicking into place. Clouds
decelerate and make like everything is normal:
the children wanting porridge, voices forcing
pattern out of circumstance, pitching rhythmic
incident on little grids of expectation, satisfaction,

disappointment, and this new awe, and walking to
school, at the corner where the halfway house is,
leaves animated in a briefest circle by the wind.

im CAEL
11.3.21

Carl Phillips

Scattered Snows, to the North

Does it matter that the Roman
Empire was still early in its slow
unwinding into never again? Then,
as now, didn't people burst into tears
in front of other people, or in private,
for no reason that they were willing
to give, or they weren't yet able to,

or for just no reason? I've never
stopped missing you, I used to
practice saying, for when I'd
need those lines, as I assumed
I would, given what I knew then –
nothing, really – about things
like love, trust, the betrayal
of trust, and a willfulness that's
only deepened inside me, all
these years, during which I can
almost say I've missed no one –
though it hurts,
                              to say it . . .

Honestly, the Roman Empire,
despite my once having studied it,
barely makes any sense to me now,
past the back-and-forthing of
patrolled borders as the gauge
and proof of hunger's addictive
and erosive powers. But there were
people, of course, too, most of them
destined to be unremembered,
who filled in their drawn lives
anyway – because what else
is there? – to where the edges
gave out. If it was night, they lit
fires, presumably. Tears
were tears.

Claire Pollard

Pollen

The medium death chose, this time, was love.
Kindness, or what we'd thought was kindness, was now harm
and it was best if we just locked ourselves away,
and didn't show we cared,
and hardly lived in weeks, which were our work.
One week, though, I recall, the pollen came,
piled in our street like snow, or no, like baby hair –
I saw a boy that stroked its fur,
how, on their walk, girls kicked at it,
its carriage on the air from home to home,
over fences, yards, the apple blossom,
in through kitchen windows
to where we stared at screens on makeshift desks;
its waver on warm currents of my breath,
how my eyes streamed with tears.
Tell me that you noticed.
And did you close the window too,
uncertain, now, what you were meant to do
with all that tenderness?

Highly Commended Poems

Qudsia Akhtar

My Dad is a Terrorist

My dad has a grey beard, pumps the car's
stereo with a man reciting Allah's words,
carries Surah Yaseen in his car's glove
compartment, eats with his right hand,
greets his neighbours, visits the mosque,
cares for the elderly, gives to charity,
prays five times a day and eats his fruit,
loves my mum's curry, has jokes up his
sleeves. He wears my mum's
prescribed glasses to read the Quran but
after he reads Surah Fatiha, he falls asleep.

Yes, that's my dad –
    the terrorist.

Will Alexander

extract from *Refracted Africa*

I see
not with the cartography of decimals
or chronicled shifts of consciousness according to conversant calculation

thinking remains a subsequent disorder
a Gargantuan artefact
kindled as secretion trapped inside limits

instead I lean towards the neural mathematics of borderless grammes

& this neural mathematics contains within the cells
emission that sustain themselves as comets

this being the Congo
other than necrosis
other than turbulent axioms
as embittered solar force

so under modern duress
I enunciate language from Radio Free Congo*
concerning elevated levels of lead in the blood remain spoiled &
          conjoined by tsetse flies

perhaps I remain curiously condensed as demonized bravery

in our eastern region
our people are thought not to have pulse
not even capable of ruin
thus the Congo carries as apostrophe nothingness
as we were a brazen cipher
arrayed with postulates of tautology

not unlike the weather that swarms near post-Neptunian objects 80,000
     AUs from the Sun*

as Congolese we replicate the impossible
our physical structure seemingly capable of the bizarre

in Western terminology we remain a dazed compounding
where our body gains no equated merit of itself

thus our desecrated carcass conjoins with raped amounts

we seek to be expunged from deficit
from our tenacious array of suffering
from our refracted blood & semen

being negation
collapsing in shadowy splinters
we weep throughout darkened intervals

via Occidental proxy points
I remain stark interior perplexity
being void
being primeval as blankness
I am concurrently a maze telepathic with outcomes
always alive according to blinding omegas

& this never quite factors
to understanding that hails from 'day to day'
plotted in language that remains as uncontested hylic

& by this hylic grammar
they seek to annihilate the atoms in me

Claire Askew

Foreplay

Usually he's quick with the *on your knees* stuff,
but tonight he starts on the hill above my house.
The dark here isn't really, on account of the stars
thick and yellow as gorse, so his loose step
on the path is fast, the sandy gravel
splashing. I hear him stop at the door and pause.

Perhaps his hand is pressed against the wood –
he's shuddering those lungs with one last
bootstrapped pull from the vape that flavours him
cinnamon, clove. He knows I'm up here
in the eaves – my brave little heart unravelled with want –
as he blows a silent howl of smoke into the night's ear.

I'll wait for the latch of his fingers in my hair, for
the quickened things he's promised as long
as I can stand. He's on the stairs now – taking them
slow as a tongue meanders up a spine,
and I'm lying on my plain bed like it's white-
hot coals, my body a hammered blade.

He's on the landing, turning out the light.
He's told me to, so I'll wait, and wait, and wait.

Polly Atkin

Monthlies

My monthlies are not
your monthlies. My monthlies
come dressed up as a 16 gauge needle
swinging an empty pint-sized tote
and a bag of saline. I am no good
with emptiness. My body wants volume.
Take take take. My monthlies insist
they are saving my life, on my body's failure
to give enough up, on my body's peculiar
habit of hoarding hot metal like stolen
trophies, stashing iron in the back
corners of all of my organs as though
I am living alone in a mansion and have to
fill every room with scrap as though
it's a pathological love of things
that brings me back to this ward, this green
vinyl bed by the french door, this plastic
pillowcase, month on month.

Sheri Benning

Plainsong

Driving home from Uncle Richard's,
             in the backseat with my brother and sister –
    weft of limbs, pearlescence of moonlit skin,
               shift and fall of their breath.

My face against the car window to watch stars, and every mile
        a farm, yard-lights,
a voice in plainsong –

           after feeding the cattle, Dave Saretzky stepping into his porch,
               borscht warming on the stove,
                    hambone, pepper, cloves.
       She's tucking in their youngest boy,
           her palm on his feverish cheek.
    After, she and Dave will sleep, in the space their bodies have learned
           to make from years of sharing
                 blood, spit, loam –

Blink of frost on wheat stalks, fields left in stubble to snare
          October's first snow-squall, the tip of dad's cigarette,
    knots of smoke, mother singing low to the radio,
           the gypsy-light of stars and farms,
           a raw harmony

like the dark wave of geese lifting off the slough just east of our barns.
    Their winter homing, a folksong for the journey
       to where flesh might belong.

Our farm's sold. Dave's too. Uncle Richard died seventeen years ago.
    Only now the light of this memory reaches me.

Fiona Benson

Edelweiss

Sometimes I walked my daughter in her pram
indoors; drew the heavy curtains so we moved
in velvet blue, then rocked her back and forth,
back and forth, to try and get her off to sleep.
She was relentless in her wakefulness,
and I was bloodshot and twitching, reeling
under the weight of my own exhaustion.
She wouldn't take a bottle, insisted on the breast.
At every painful station of the night
I prised myself from sleep, dreams sluicing off
my skin, brought her into bed, and sat up shivering
to feed her, the mouth for whom my body was made.
The muscles of my neck kept easing, snapping back:
exhausted puppet, doll-head. Afraid
I'd smother her, or drop her, afraid to sleep.
In the middle of the day I'd wheel her
in the second-hand, Victorian-style pram
that lurched along on its shot suspension,
as its capacious black hood slipped inevitably back
like a broken concertina, a retracting fan.
How I loathed the thing: its thoughtless summoning
of the nineteenth-century's infant dead,
its black bassinet like a hearse, and our baby girl
staring up from its deep bed with her vast dark eyes
shining and alert, as if she felt my fears
and didn't mean to sleep. That day, I wanted a lullaby
to soothe us both but couldn't recall a song,
couldn't remember being sung to,
and sadness was upon me as I faltered
on the only hush-thing I could improvise,
'Edelweiss' – the same two half-remembered lines
crooned over and over again, a fragment of song

for a tiny flower, its gleaming shred.
All round me the dark was rising tenderly:
our false-created night, its texture and felted weft
thickening like an alpine meadow, its softly flowered grass,
and I was falling in its dark blue lush, its reservoir of stars
as my Grandma Bairstow, who'd been dead for years,
took my hands off the pram and laid me down
to rest, then began to wheel her great-granddaughter,
who seemed to know her, and resumed the song;
she knew all the words, knew all the sore
and phosphorescent work of raising children,
how mothers move in the dark like shining wounds,
like gaps in being. She sang, and all the hurt
and beautiful universe, all the souls
came crowding in.

Emily Berry

Scholar

I had a close friend who was a scholar of unbelief. Once she interviewed me for her study and identified me as a believer in symbols. She had a designated category for this type of person, which I forget. I did not like to think of myself as belonging to a category. Yet I later encountered many other people who fell into it – they were often poets. For example, I set great store by the proverb about magpies. If I saw a single magpie it was not that I thought bad luck would befall me, but I saw the bird as symbolic of the sorrow that had blighted my life. It was a confirmation. Now the sorrow was accounted for, and it was beautiful, because magpies were. They had that deep indigo stripe among the black.

Clíodhna Bhreathnach

Aughrim Street Doomscroll

Who are those crows? Do watching Black & Tans
still nest up on these roofs? My timeline glows
with posts of other poets winning grants.
I look up at the scaffolded night, the co-
living schemes half-built, then pass
the church, a sign with shout of WET PAINT
hanging still from its syrup-black gates.
A bloom of air in my mouth's blue mask,
I float down the street's brick stream
a living bog-body. A passing Garda grunts
and I stare back, a crowning lump
up my throat of gone-off screams –
I am two fools, I know, for despairing,
& for saying so, in fucking poetry.

Sam Buchan-Watts

Lines following

> '*I have set you here*'

On the way into the woods, do you feel someone
turn the focus of the lens with the topmost parts
of their forefinger and thumb –
in line with the crick of your neck, as you turn to look
but feel the head fixed straight. The branches tick,
someone set them going. The woods have set you here,
so as to feel away from thoughts, but still you think
I never really entered. The way into the woods is in a way
to go round the woods: the woods are always in the way
when you're in them (if they're woods). The way in
weighs on the memory of summer like a cloak hung
over the sun. The way in is an act of hyphenation,
a statement about the weather, the weather in the woods.

Victoria Adukwei Bulley

Declaration (I)

check if you want to

    but you won't find any

        lyric shame here.

            we don't do that, no;

                we nuh ave dat here.

                    you won't find one lash

                        on the surface of this eye –

                            look: if I say I, I mean

                                a lot of people

                                    & at this table

                                        all of us eat

Joe Carrick-Varty

From the Perspective of Coral

An exhibition in seven rooms

There are a large number of particulates suspended
in the ocean, and while suicide does not
have eyelashes to keep particulates out of its eyes
as humans do, it emits a certain frequency
(some call it a hum, a toothache,
the background wind of a 4am voicemail)
which continuously bathes the eye
with an oily protein mucus.

*

Considered one of the least-known
and rarest living things, suicide
is hardly ever seen with the naked eye
except last week in Morrison's when
reaching for a mango, opening
a box of eggs
to check for cracks.

*

Suicide needs to see
in a wide range of light levels.
Anyone who has gone scuba diving knows
the difficulties of underwater vision.
Visibility can be affected by the turbidity of water
and the deeper you get
the less light penetrates and you slowly
lose colours.

*

I'd like to draw your attention to slide 7
'Suicide Suspended', as seen from the ocean floor
(from the perspective of coral).
It is unclear as to whether suicide is ascending
or descending. It is unclear as to whether
suicide is alone or calling to a mate.

*

I'd like you to imagine the deepest,
widest body of water you can.

Anne Carson

extract from *H of H Playbook*

Theseus [voiceover]
The thing you have to understand is,
not half these people realize they're in
a myth. You know what this reminds
me of, this commodity fetish, this H of
H, reminds me of the way Melville talks
about the sperm whale – "the
skeleton…articulated throughout so
that, like a great chest of drawers you
can open and shut him, in all his bony
cavities – spread out his ribs like a
gigantic fan and swing all day upon his
lower jaw" – I'm just saying, let's be
careful. This whale isn't dead. But he'd
like to be, is why I'm here. He saved me
once. I owe him.

He hides his head. They always hide
their head when the fight goes out of
them. When they can't reach their own
beautiful ideas anymore and the birds
keep dying on the windshield and the
gods have the phone off the hook. Yet
I admit H of H was a special case.
Maybe no rougher than anyone else as
to background and he was ever a crazy
pony in early days, off on a gallop at
every wind, fixated on a white pickup
truck for one whole summer, whoa that
was stupid, but then he got involved in
an action he calls The Labours. Ten
years there. Ten years a long time.

Who knows what really went on. When the war is over turn out the lights, we used to say (or was it a song) but you don't wak out of ten years of Labours into normal living. You eat like a bulldozer, get drunk too easy, get angry too fast, get yourself lost, go ice blue all night. God, night is bad. Main thing is you hate fear. Fear is a sin. I'm just saying, let's not break connexion with him. This river has no third side. So I go up close. I say, H of H, look at me, unwrap your head.

Maya Caspari

Mixed Other

I came to whiteness like a spill
Whiteness seemed to me
wanting smoothness. It was sound
white noise. Whiteness was
here, a family video
Whiteness came to me like cling film
to skin, wrinkling mostly at
you were related. Whiteness was
claiming precision, cut
of sky to water
an edge,
breathing silence,
nothing to see
waving lines of static.
shiny, stretched, stuck
contact. *I didn't know*
a hiding texture, coy
only just for you

Whiteness was a room
a changing room of
part of me, meaning me in
changing weight,
wanting to watch without witness
like plane entrails dissecting sky and
marking not quite undone
torn holes in air,
and both; my sky, pale belly and
a hole aching an archive
holding *what?*, lines
spilling slowly
changing at each touch,
lockered layers, holding apart
not me. Whiteness was a
wanting clearness, wanting *look* –,
Whiteness was a slipping claim,
sky almost dissolving lines of flight
that part of you's –
– *all gone* my being *and*
its navel ozone cut
moving, peeling,
piling up and
out of air

Anna Cheung

Monster Tinder

I'll lay footprints, white and silent,
deep in your heart.

                              Bigfoot
Swipe left

Unwrap my bandaged body,
undress my eyes and untie my hands.
Let me release my lips all over you.

                              Tutankhamun
Swipe left

Let's watch the moon ripen together
beyond the owls and midnight trees,
and I'll unleash my inner animal.

                              Werewolf
Swipe right

Touch here; my chest is ajar
– red raw arteries loosened
from stitches when I fell for you.

                              Frankenstein
Swipe left

The scent of your neck
drowns me in bloodlust and heat.
Let me be the nail in your coffin.

                            Dracula

Swipe right

                    IT'S A MATCH!

Rohan Chhetri

King's Feedery

After the rape & the bloodbath, the savage king
& his men retired to a long shed built in an open
field by a thin river fashioned for this lull in the pillaging
so the horses could rest. One by one, they scrubbed
blood off their fingers & faces & sat down to devour
a feast of rice & goat served by the villagers.
The legend remains only in the name of a lodge
built in the same place, which from the Bengali means
the King's Feedery, where the king took his meal.
We say Death stays here when it visits someone
in the family. The time it came for Grandfather, it arrived
late. Not at the wolf's hour between midnight & first
light, but late morning on the highway, siren blaring
all the way to the nursing home. As if punishing us
for what it botched, it hung around for a few
months at the Feedery, then came for my aunt. Young,
suffering in a marriage, she was taken straight by her weak
heart. I imagine them, father & daughter, sitting still
across a table, sharing a meal of steaming boiled potatoes,
& always in the afterlife that vague dream of salt.
Death takes in threes, they said. We feared it would
come for one of us. In the trashed room,
they found Death's ledger full of illegible scrawls
in a dark meter no one could understand.
Grandmother's devastation circled complete, that year
a channel of clear water began thrumming beneath
her skin. We heard it rumble whenever she opened
her mouth to speak. When I think of love,

I think of her weeping as I left, her swollen lip
grazing the back of my hand through the car window. Brief
& bright her long blurred life now summoned
with Death lurking at the borders again.
Married at thirteen, adolescence lost
weeping into a cauldron of chopped onions. She talks
of the flimsy wooden hovel perched on four
frayed stumps & in her telling it is always
how she saw it first, herself decked in gold
with that sinking dread: a preface. I think of love
& I think how when they lifted Grandfather's bier
she called out to him crying   *My child*
my god   my child

Carolyn Jess Cooke

Things Will Work Out

Things will work out.
Maybe not today, which has sadness
running through it like ore,
the mineral-tasting wind knocking cans
across the street and the disconsolate sea
banging its head off the desk.

You wonder where all the fog has come from.
Not the fog that creeps
in every September,
smudging the streetlights, but one
that's been made
from the scraps of your life.

The fears you believe in – *know* – are
coiling around your heart, your lungs,
building up a muscle
you don't realise you have. Somewhere
beyond here, a river is bending to velvety stones
along the bank, listening to their news.

On the hillside where you used to play
spears of emerald grass are folding
under the weight of rain. Jewel by jewel,
water passes to the earth, and the blades
straighten to sun again. A storm fritters
to breath. Traffic gathers. Things will work out.

Alex Dimitrov

Sunset on 14th Street

I don't want to sound unreasonable
but I need to be in love immediately.
I can't watch this sunset
on 14th Street by myself.
Everyone is walking fast
right after therapy, texting back
their lovers orange hearts
and unicorns—it's insane to me.
They're missing this free sunset
willingly! Or even worse
they're going home to cook
and read this sad poem online.
Let me tell you something,
people have quit smoking.
They don't get drinks
but they juice. There are
way too many photos
and most all of us look better
in them than we do in life.
What happened? This is
truly so embarrassing!
I want to make a case
for 1440 minutes every day
where we stop whatever else
is going on and look each other
in the eyes. Like dogs.
Like morning newspapers
in evening light. So long!
So much for this short drama.
We will die one day
and our cheap headlines
won't apply to anything.

The internet will be forgotten.
All the praise and pandering.
I'd really rather take a hike
and by the way, I'm gay.
The sunset too is homosexual.
At least today, between
the buildings which are moody
and the trees (which honestly)
they look a bit unhealthy here.
They're anxious. They're concerned.
They're wondering why
I'm broke and lonely
in Manhattan—though of course
I'll never say it—and besides
it's almost spring. It's fine.
It's goth. Hello! The truth is
no one will remember us.
We're only specks of dust
or one—one speck of dust.
Some brutes who screamed
for everything to look at us.
Well, look at us. Still terrible
and awful. Awful and pretending
we're not terrible. Such righteous
saints! Repeating easy lines,
performing our great politics.
It's just so very boring,
the real mystery in fact
is how we managed to make room
for love at all. Punk rock,
avant-garde cinema.
I love you, reader
but you should know
the sunset's over now.

I'm standing right in front of
Nowhere bar, dehydrated
and quite scared
but absolutely willing
to keep going. It makes sense
you do the same. It's far
too late for crying and quite
useless too. You can be sad
and still look so good. You can
say New York is beautiful
and it wouldn't be a headline
and it wouldn't be a lie.
Just take a cab and not the 6,
it's never once in ten years
been on time. It's orbiting
some other world
where there are sunsets
every hour and no money
and no us—that's luck!
The way to get there
clearly wasn't written down.
Don't let that stop you though.
Look at the sky. Kiss everyone
you can for sure.

Mark Fiddes

Hotel Petroleum

Dear Guest,

Your air-conditioning is the voice of love.
It sighs and cools like cotton sheets.
Each pool reflects your inner turquoise.
All that you touch is fragrant and labial.
Even the trees are squeezed for perfume.
Your limbs tan the suede of antelopes.
You feel as thin as your platinum card.
Your eyes take on whatever sky you desire.
Diamonds crust your lovely skull inside,
lighting up your brain like a film set.
Conscience will be supplied by Pokémon.
Your ragged past we dumped in the sand
with all the other non-refundable rubbish.
Your future we desalinate for freshness.
Your anxiety you may feed to the birds
whose volume knob is next to your bed.
The on-off button is for self-control.
What you don't have, you may shop for,
even Virtue, with its bold new branding
and an exciting user interface to die for.
Until the humming stops, the power dies
and stars arrive to mock the endless night
just say yes to everything. Thank you.

Jay Gao

Imperium Abecedarian

Oh! Adventurer

Oh! Boss

Oh! Coloniser

Oh! Despot

Oh! Emperor

Oh! Fascist

Oh! God

Oh! Hero

Oh! Imperator

Oh! Jailer

Oh! King

Oh! Leader

Oh! Monarch

Oh! Nazi

Oh! Overlord

Oh! Pioneer

Oh! Queen

Oh! Ruler

Oh! Sovereign

Oh! Translator

Oh! Usurper

Oh! Voyeur

Oh! Wanderer

Oh! Xénos

Oh! You

Oh! Zealot

let us start the clock

Louise Glück

Poem

Day and night come
hand in hand like a boy and a girl
pausing only to eat wild berries out of a dish
painted with pictures of birds.

They climb the high ice-covered mountain,
then they fly away. But you and I
don't do such things—

We climb the same mountain;
I say a prayer for the wind to lift us
but it does no good;
you hide your head so as not
to see the end—

Downward and downward and downward and downward
is where the wind is taking us;

I try to comfort you
but words are not the answer;
I sing to you as mother sang to me—

Your eyes are closed. We pass
the boy and girl we saw at the beginning;
now they are standing on a wooden bridge;
I can see their house behind them;

How fast you go they call to us,
but no, the wind is in our ears,
that is what we hear—

And then we are simply falling—

And the world goes by,
all the worlds, each more beautiful than the last;

I touch your cheek to protect you—

Roz Goddard

Small Moon Curve

Small moon curve, warm in my hand,
rising like a sweet bun. In another life

you would slip, wet with kisses from a silk
dress, sleep as a small animal through

a yellow afternoon. It's dawn.
Sunrise milks the skylight.

We're dressing in backless gowns,
ivory stockings. Oh, to hear a blackbird.

My wedding ring slides onto a finger of air.
The surgeon asks me to name my future.

You're performing a left breast mastectomy.
He touches my shoulder the way a bird lands,

feels ice under its feet, inks a cross near
the thickening. Each woman he visits sings her

own winter. We're a grove of tenderness as trees
in sorrow are. Two nurses walk me to theatre,

ask how I usually spend mornings. I mention
watching corvids, pot-bellied in oaks, listening

to their love songs from another realm.
I've lived the life of two crows.

Hannah Hodgson

What Happened?

For those of us who live inside the air hangar, stripped down
for parts and sold; there's another dozen who sell their bodies whole.

I pawned my liver to a bear so he could feed his children.
My lungs were gifted to an Aurelian, who pinned them

next to other moths. I sold my radius to a medical student
needing experience in fractures. I auctioned my left elbow

to an aristocrat who put it next to his taxidermied caterpillar.
My shoulder is betrothed to a creepy dressmaker,

and this morning my bicep fell out, a fish now clubbed.
I stuff newspaper into the gaps left.

Padding my skin, a cabinet of slowly disappearing valuables.

Sarah James

Marcasite

The watch Nan gave me never worked
longer than a few weeks. The trick,
she reminded me, was to keep it wound,

but not over-wind it. Whatever colour
her wig, Nan's curls were always sleek
and tight. She'd clutch my wrist, tell me

I was her favourite – her first, prized,
eldest great-grandchild, though perhaps
she said likewise to my sister and cousins.

She smiled, toothy as a polished watch-cog,
even as she grew thinner and shorter,
even as she out-survived one daughter.

Her intricate silver-linked watch
hangs loosely on my wrist, unticking.
I finger the strap; each tiny marcasite

still shines as brightly as her eyes did.

Lisa Kelly

Red Data List of Threatened British Fungi: Mainly Smuts

Smut, lie down with me in annual meadow grass that tickles
our pelts. Smut, be barley covered and reeking of beer,
a bearberry redleaf prim on each pinkish part. Smut, with your bedstraw hair,
bestow no interloper a bird's eye view. My promise, a primrose
with its fairy caretaker that no bog asphodel, no bone-breaker
will I brook, smut. As a chick weeds out a worm, I will weed out
all burrowing doubts, all jealousies, all winter green looks
on our love, smut, which would shrivel us, smut. Smut, be not false.
This oat-grass ring, I twine about your finger, smut.
Think of me when a foxtail, smut, lifts to expose a gland,
stinking of March violets, to deceive you, smut.
They'd have you frogbit, smut, back in the pond where you
were spawned, mounted and belly grasped. Glaucus sedge creeps
in damp ditches, smut. Weep for such green hell bore away
with earth's daughter, smut. Loose your hair. See how sedge flowers in spikelets,
smut, and love always pricks. Lie down with me in meadow grass that tickles
our pelts. Revel in mudwort, smut. I could call you close to Limosella, smut,
cloaked in tiny white stars, a northern bilberry redleaf prim on each pinkish part.
Passion marks us, smut, with a purple small-reed stripe, smut.
My rare spring sedge, smut, tender as fresh shoots.
My reed canary-grass, smut, sensitive to noxious airs. Saxifrage smut,
I cannot help but repeat saxifrage smut, the brassy instrument of you played.
Sing of prickly yuletide, sea holly smut. They are small spored
with their white beaks, sedge smut, poking and prodding and stinking, smut.
They are not sweet – they confuse carnal with vernal, smut.
Damn the white beak-sedge, smut, worn by quacks as if we were plague, smut,
with their aromatic herbs, smut. What rare pathogens we are, smut.
What gall smut, to detest our dark teliospores. Yellow toadflax
on them all, the cowards that croak. Yellow toadflax on them all, smut.

Zaffar Kunial

The Wind in the Willows

Although the book was another country to me
I knew the title and the title stuck. I always
liked the title. The species too. I'd say, if asked,
it was my favourite kind of tree, though it was never
with one certain tree in mind. There was a garden

I vaguely remember, the way the leaves curtained
like shadows. A lit cave. A fringe, not yours, you could
look through. And the supple wood made cricket
bats, which was a part of the little I also knew.
Maybe it was all a little to do with letters too,

two tongueless trees of *ll*, the uncrowing big *W*s
in *The Wind in the Willows*; maybe it was all aural – in
the echoed 'in', *Wind in* . . . the *the*s . . . the three billowy *w*s –
maybe the leaf-fringed mystery, between the two.
And speaking of poetry, I had this initiating thought

that the flax-smelling willow in the first cricket bat
I was gifted, contained the wind, held old power still.
Light enough, slight arms could lift it. Wind in willow,
this percussive wood a gathered strength. A mutual
bind. Though I was far from writing – or this book –

that sense, I suppose in spirit, was poetry and early.

The very last thing poetry is

is a poem.

Mukahang Limbu

The Day

will come like a breath when you refuse
any negotiations on your body, your eyes
stop being a lighthouse for compliments about

how good your English is, your smile can take
that weekend off, kick back and choose
any seat it likes. Your politeness will remain

in your pocket, no longer a passport,
and your skin will stop being an entry
on a colour chart that has no name for

the brow of a Himalayan sunrise or the shade
of rain on an egg-fried-rice afternoon, or the
powder of a bleeding temple. One day white

people won't skim this poem about your
body, they will have learned to listen to a
sea that isn't a tremulous roar of pebbles,

to see some sky that isn't theirs, a river of litter
running to a plastic beach, a difficult
breeze, they will hear those vehicles rattling

on an earthquake road, the laugh of a landscape,
houses filled with monsoon green, flowers,
dogs barking, the cries and laughter of a body

that's mine

Fran Lock

Hyena Q & A

Q: And what's it *like* being a hyena?

A: It is like withdrawal, trembling its traces all across the
splendid belly of the night. It is ecstatic and mechanical,
a kind of sanguinary prickling, to be made spectral with
adrenaline, to stream raw light through your fibre optic
veins. It is holding the ice of his name in my mouth until it
cools. Until, I mean, it thaws.

Q: How has being a hyena affected your employment
prospects?

A: Imagine having a clubfoot. Except it isn't your foot, it's
your whole body. Imagine a woman's face eaten away by
radiation. That's how people look at you, a cheesy fifties
pinup, her thighs tempered with ugly ragged holes.

Q: But *do* you work?

A: I practice walking upright. I type with a hollow wand
between my teeth, a tango-dancer's wilting rose.

Q: Have hyenas many friends?

A: Spotted hyenas travel in packs, like non-league football supporters. A strand wolf is rarer, androgynous thicket, a sweating maze of hair. A strand wolf forms a band in college, is sad, stratospheric and doomed, likes to be looked at, never touched. The striped hyena is *not* musical, will wear a big-ass garland of garlic bulbs to keep at bay all vampires.

Q: Vampires?

A: The opposite of *hyena* is not *human*. The opposite of *hyena* is *vampire*.

Q: Does a hyena ever take a lover?

A: *Thistles* are not *thorns*. There is no *thorn soup*, just as there is no *hyena love*. Sex is a wet ghost, solicitous and pitiful, his thin mouth open like the meekest wound. There was a *sweetheart* once, exemplary gelatine, the sugared whorls of her haunches dissolved in milky tea.

Q: What kind of answer is that?

A: What would you have me say? There were dauntless boys, doubly gone, and a girl who spoke in maudlin strophes the briny savour of *suicide*. A hyena bears her own irreparable juju. A hyena is both the Jonah and the boat.

Q: Are you trying to tell me something?

A: Yes, like Sappho.

Q: Are *all* hyenas lesbians?

A: Some people have a way of saying *lesbian*, like a foot being stamped at a children's party. Your eyes are the most indiscriminate blue, like the faulty jizzing flames of an electrical fire. I do not desire you. I do not desire. Neither grunt and thrust nor coax and yearn. Picture Valerie Solanas swooning in a field of wheat. You can't, can you? There is no *thorn wine* either.

Q: Does a hyena know when she will die?

A: Yes, in the grime of twilight, fermenting a requiem among the rotten apples. They will build a shrine to me beside Camden Canal, but it will be inaccessible except by kayak. On the third day of my death, I will perform my first miracle.

Q: Does it bother you that you are such a tiresome person?

A: On my way here a line of gaunt yellow flowers, my crude little comrades, who fizz with wiry life. Do they give a shit that people think they're weeds?

Q: But are you *really* a hyena?

A: I have rubbed myself along the surface of the world. Extinction is a coal sewn into my belly. I put it there on purpose. A hyena is a punch-line in search of a joke.

Amelia Loulli

Holy Water

'So everything will live where the river goes.'
  Ezekiel 47:9

The river is on fire. Somewhere near a moonless industrial unit in Merseyside,
  where they dispose of her remains. The river is pure
paraffin. The river is a sea of flames, a labyrinth of flammable swimming spots.
  The river will never be the same again. The river has never
known such heat. The river is more fluid now than it's ever been. The river
  is a rippling depth of pyrotechnics. The river is blazing.
The river is incapable of putting itself out, an incendiary water way. The river
  will set fire to this whole godforsaken place. The river
is reflecting its own brilliant orange blue. The river is a fire in a mirror, a torch
  of veins. The river is a beautiful, monstrous truth. The river
is a tinder box, dry with its own desperate retching. Don't you think it wants
  to bring even one tiny thing back? Don't you think God
would be impressed by a whole body so sorry, so fierce it has learnt to become
  a fuel, to strike a match, to hold its own breath?

Lila Matsumoto

All of the pans in the kitchen

All of the pans in the kitchen were being used to boil cauliflowers,
submerging the house in a deep mephitic funk. He showed me
around, entirely relaxed in attitude, lord of the duplex. A sort of
constant humming emanated from his body, even as he spoke,
producing curious and not entirely unpleasant overtones. I had
the strong impression that he was an experimental ventriloquist.
On top of the dining table was a weightlifting bench because, he
said, one should always exercise with altitude. In the end I turned
down the lodgings. I couldn't imagine the musical group he
insisted we form, as housemates.

Lucy Mercer

Imago

I walk up to a black bucket
full of water and full of an image,
it's a reflection again

if I could see above, it would not
startle me.

we are in an invisible harness,
Andrea,
but it's only with asymmetries

like water distorting in a bucket
like the shock of being entered by another
like a birthday that was easier last year –
that we can believe we are moving.

this is the beloved who walks around and closes
the eyes of carnations in the air.

Jake Morris-Campbell

Each Pebble Its Part

Not my North

North   My North

Every word I put down
every line break
stanza, sequence – not enough

Basil, your Northern landscapes
are not my Northern landscapes

I'm here at Marsden Bay
with two elderly dogs
the only girl I've ever thought to marry
two hundred miles away

You are dead and you cannot help me

I write of the swift flight of spuggy
thinking – as you didn't – of Bede

How do I live in a place
whose sparrows
are in terminal decline?

Some days it is easier to remember
than to live

I have amputated
myself into
a life
I partially inhabit.

As for love –
sometimes a cwtch means more
than hiraeth or hyem

Basil, your Northern landscapes
are not my Northern landscapes

And these days we drown in the bogus

Wired up in ways
you'd barely comprehend
making notes in your Moleskin
on the train to Wylam

If there is such thing as a 'poet's vision'
then let me seize it—
Hoy this phone, this laptop into the Tyne
and I will not decline
to walk, to log, to legislate
my true North, true Love
truly gan hyem

My North   North   Not my North

My brother and sister say they'd never come
back
if none of our family lived here

We are one marriage or job away from exile

I have thought
to pick up each pebble
on Shields beach

What would it mean to lose the sand
        strip away each grain?
                        I have thought about my mates
                        pulled by the sodium glare
                of middle English towns
            so far from the smell of the sea

Pulled like iron filings
        to the magnetic thrust
                        of The City

                            I have thought
What would it mean

                At slack tide
        Your poem burns too bright.
            How should I write?

                Each

    Pebble   its

            Part.

Briancia Mullings

Queen's Speech

It was mama who taught me, mi please and mi thank-yous,
And small island who taught I my vowels
Dem a call it colloquial, slang
It's my tongue
But mi cyant speak like dem no more now

'This is Queen's speech, England,
Proper way and proper talk.'
De right way, colonised way
Deny your race like issa sport

My 'h's', my accent
Were indigenous to mi throat
Swallow down hard British water, till your 'h's' begin to float,
Till you ah choke
On the tip of your tongue,
Wid vowels in de gaps of your teeth
Dem a foreign, dem uncivilised
Dem nah talk like ah we

And in only three years
Did dem manage to tame
Mi wild native tongue
Buried in de back of my brain

That jungle like roar, mi speech would pronounce
Hibernates in de fluid of my cerebral doubt
Whitewashed and white drowned
Lungs filled wid invasion
Puffing up my wind box to talk with occasion

Queen's Speech
Most formal, and most eloquent a pitch.
Buoyant fluid words that escape out just in to fit.
Yet I progress to feel morbidly alone,
England is not all just London, no Queen's speech fluid tone

To evolve and to adapt to an international tongue.
Just as I struggle wid both
Mi cyant identify just wid one

It was mama who taught mi how to switch on and off at my
core
So, mi used to speak wid Vincy dialect
But I can't speak like that anymore.

Molly Naylor

The Worries

When I was a child I'd lie in bed with
the *Big Break* theme tune stuck in my head
and Rolodex through my worries
like a burnt-out businesswoman.
My dolls were mean girls from school,
my sheets sandpapered my skin.

One night my dad came in,
and shy under my Lego fringe,
I spread my worries out across my bed.
So serious, he couldn't not laugh
but he let me keep the night light on.

I sometimes think if I'd been less afraid
I could have gone so far.
Had breakfast in more countries,
slept in beds across the world,
bumped into those mean girls from school
in Cornish pubs, and greeted them like Spring.

Although I suppose it's possible that I've
gone and done as much
as I was ever going to do.
Maybe the worries stopped me doing more
or maybe everywhere I went,
the worries took me there.

Eiléan Ní Chuilleanáin

What happened next?

So, will we ever be told what happened afterwards
to the man who had fallen among thieves
as he went down from Jerusalem to Jericho:
half killed, what happened to him
after the Samaritan paid for his care at the inn?

Or what became of the women in Naples in 1944
who sold rough sex to soldiers in public for food,
their faces never changing as they took it?
How can I even ask, who would I ask? Indeed,
it was never the point of the story.

Fiction or truth, it will be told again:
This happened in my lifetime in a place I know –
the moment the light falls on the victim and then
it moves away slowly, the light
that also falls when there's nobody there to see it.

When I begin the telling the words will not be quiet,
I have to lie down beside them and listen
to the crackling syllables that keep beginning again
each time the wheel of language spins,

but they never tell what happened after the ending.
They have so many stories, and not all
have been heard already, and not all of them
can tell us clearly what we ought to have done.

Eugene Ostashevsky

We are trying to make sense

We are trying to make sense of a feeling.

Making sense of a feeling is like building a boat from water.

Feeling is a field. It is uneven. None of its points is like any other.

A field of what. A field of being afield. Afield of what. Afield of being a field.

Or feeling is fieldwork. For it involves an other.

When it does not involve another, it is called fooling.

Even when it does involve another, it may still be called fooling.

It never fully involves another.

To fight against fooling we think of feeling as feeling about.

Feeling about means trying to touch the object of your feeling.

It is often done in the dark. We feel about when we cannot see and grasp.

How do we feel about each other.

We feel for each other. We feel for each other in the dark.

We feel for each other in the dark, trying to make sense of the feeling.

Stuti Pachisia

Boys Over Flowers

You tell me you are engaging in a Twitter War,
capital T, capital W. I open the thread and
you have said please and thank you and agree to disagree.

I think of men with leather boots, spiked studs,
blue overalls, covered in dust. A red rose, settled
by the ear. One of my favourite questions to ask boys

is what their favourite flower is. A boy once
told me it was a cactus, and I was willing to spend
half my money on buying a joke present for a joke answer,
half-hoping he was half-joking.

I never thought of asking you. Instead, I remember you sitting
by lavender, by the stream, your hands: too big, your smile: too wide,
turning the night starry and lavender-scented

simply by existing. It isn't like

you are delicate. It isn't like you can be plucked apart and
put back together, in the desperation of willing love, in a game of
does he, doesn't he.

It isn't like when I think of magenta lilies, I think
of boys unscrewing jars and laughing in the kitchen,
a hot sauce bubbling.

It isn't like when the stalks of sunflowers turn white
and smell like cinnamon tea, I think
of boys snipping perfect paper dolls, eight

a sheet. Instead, it is more like

I think of your salmon shirt. The one you have never worn in front
of me, each time I cut open a watermelon. It is more like

I think of you harmonizing, purring from your chest, each time
I wake to a garden buzzing. It is more like

I can see your hands erupt into flowers, your feet sprouting leaves,
your elbows browning, your neck scarred like trees,

each time you fight for fairness, and still
end with please.

Mark Pajak

The Tilt

Those days when Mum's hangover
was a dark kitchen, sat at the table,
head in her hands like a full bowl,

I'd slip out of the house and come here:
this bookshop on Luke Street.
In here I could shut the world

with a door and be walled in by hardbacks,
their spines full of broken capillaries.
Paperbacks neat as piano keys.

In here it was quiet. Floorboards
tense as a frozen lake. The book
in my chest that opened and closed.

And I'd kneel to a low shelf,
choose at random and break open
a loaf of paper. It didn't matter

that I couldn't afford it, or that soon
the owner would make me leave,
or that I was only four and couldn't read.

The smell of an old book is a memory of trees.
A boy can tilt into it, the way a drunk
tilts her glass, and lean back emptied.

Anita Pati

Train Triolet (16.46 to Brighton)

I won't blow you up because I'm brown,
O twitchy woman who grassed up my shopping.
I went to the loo not to twiddle my belt.
I won't blow you up because I'm brown.
Terrorists don't tend to buy Cath Kidston
unless I am a cleanskin moron.
Because I'm brown, I won't blow you up,
O *native* woman who grassed up my shopping.

Ayesha Raees

When I was a child...

When I was a child but not much considered a child, my mother said that on the day of judgement, no one would care about the other, no parent for their child, no friend for their friend, no lover for their lover. *Will you forget me too?* I asked her. *It's inevitable*, my mother replied, *you will forget me too.*

Denise Riley

What are you working on?

Someone will ask me
'What are you working on?'
On nothing, I'll say. To be
worked *on* – that'd be luck –

such 'being worked on'
could throw out a rare spark
from the language-engine's
indifferent grinding.

Its own reverbs tune
some dispassionate jabber
tweezing white noise from
a skull's ric-rac sutures.

Or am I tone-deaf to
old radio frequencies
in the glare of this stillness
that waits, incurious –

but no lament's needed
should a human receiver
fail to bear that light
clatter where no ear is.

Denise Saul

Golden Grove

i.m. Aubrey

Unbearable as night from which sleep comes,
you are everywhere at once: in the wind
on sunken earth   in stilling water.
I carry your heavy urn to Golden Grove
where tamarind trees emerge as woods.

The dream holds back day from night.
And you, a wanderer, could not wait
to leave rain behind in our city.
You will now become a thousand things:
scent of jasmine   salted air   troubling light.

Peter Scapello

Nerve

Everything I value in my life I owe to queerness. Subvert stigma, make it joy. I started scoring as regular at fifteen, for partying. Junk, my education in limits; giving people what they wanted of me and withholding traits that felt less celebratory, were fixed. The dread even saying it could conjure. So I partied, a placeholder of the self I longed to be. And continued celebrating, for something which hasn't happened yet. Using as to flirt with suicide, an incrementally sought sadness. Of course, the sex was its natural progression. Filter to anger, controllable ether. Peaking in park bushes, dirt of a public toilet; the grime that heightens throb and thrill. Shame is if anything a badge-wearing activity, inner surfacing outward. A bad flower. The losers I've fucked, an accessory. What is a void but the area between agonising and permission? Desire cannot be questioned in hindsight; suffered, ergo sinned. Now quit teasing, call me faggot for my own pleasure. In the throes there is no risk assess, no pathology. To cope is queer authority. How badly I needed you when I was drunk in the sun and closeted.

Elisabeth Sennitt Clough

The Black Dress

It's a hungry creature,
wants to devour a girl.

When the relatives make her put it on,
it shudders itself over her head.

But the girl thinks it's inviting,
in a sleeping-bag kind of way –

how the contours of her body
warm to its darkness.

Greta Stoddart

Flowers for my ego and a dark stage

with a single beam of light
  not on me I hasten to add
   but a dream I have
    where I'm curled right down
     in a corner of the universe
      and what's crowding me out
       what's bearing down on me
        while I'm being the only living thing
       down there in space
      is a vast dark mind
       I'm given to understand
       over time is mine
        and that foetal floating lost thing
        no one will ever find
       is me who I was
       before I came
      to play the part
      I was born to play
     so tell me
      who is that
       smiling and bowing
        in the vast dark hall
         wondering where everyone's gone
         and where the fuck are my flowers?

Anastasia Taylor-Lind

Welcome to Donetsk

You teach me this wartime trick –
to look for living pot plants
in the windows on Kievska Avenue.
Most are crisped and brown.

But one green geranium
and a succulent spider plant
offer proof of life
for the person who waters them.

Whole apartment blocks are abandoned.
Collapsed telephone lines,
blown-up branches
litter the road.

No voices,
no tinkering metalwork in the distance,
no buses, no playing children.
Leaves rustle white noise.

You say *It's like Sunday, every day*.
Stray dogs and swallows,
and the soft thud of shelling.

In a town recently re-taken by the Army I buy a postcard
of Donetsk on a summer evening. Rose bushes fill the
foreground. A couple arm in arm on a paved promenade gaze
out over a river, like shepherds on the hillside of a painting.

It's picture postcard perfect. Photoshopped. Probably staged.
Here, Donetsk looks like my home town. No combatants, no
soldiers, no separatists, no rebels, no terrorists, no volunteers,
no protestors, no refugees, no collateral damage, no civilian
casualties.

In newspaper photographs Donetsk resembles Grozny in
the nineties. There, war is only checkpoints, flags on the
town hall, men in mismatched combat fatigues, empty
supermarkets, curfews and families fractured by the frontline.
Smashed dinner sets, blown-out windows, shrapnel in the
vegetable patch, closed banks, cash under the bed and cars
filled with belongings.

Olly Todd

Tides

If that's the pavement rolling towards us
Through the art department phone box like a tide,
It follows that the focus puller's glove
Turns out to be lunar gravity.

The phone box is a man standing in the swash,
Riveted together, filled with a conversation,
Willing his abdicating collapse onto dry sand,
Something like phone-in radio to cut out the one

Sage-sounding chirrup in the dawn chorus,
The softly clicking clasps of makeup boxes.
If only we were as straight-backed and pomaded,
As sure about wine, as gastrically muscular

When pecking prosciutto-wrapped melon off a fork
Or biting a ghost from the air above some stairs,
Peddling a boat over fetched surf cradling
A rivet gun; strange for a tool eh?

Jessica Traynor

Anatomy Scan

Let's begin with a shroud, darkened by time,
pushed aside to show your bones' filigree.
The ultrasound probes and digs as you slither
in and out of focus, sockets gaping
like a Halloween ghost through a sheet.
The hole of your stomach. The chomp
of your heartbeat hungering below my gut.
Perfect cerebellum. A very nice spine.
There – the kidneys. Little dark pockets of need.
Colour flares across the screen, arterial flow
through widening chambers, its rush exhausting.
The eyeball's orbit. Closed but watchful.
Your twig arms flinch and flick. Your tiny jaws grin.
Little lizard. You know something I've forgotten.

Ocean Vuong

Tell Me Something Good

You are standing in the minefield again.
Someone who is dead now

told you it is where you will learn
to dance. Snow on your lips like a salted

cut, you leap between your deaths, black as god's
periods. Your arms cleaving

the wind. You are something made, then made
to survive – which means you are somebody's son.

Which means if you open your eyes, you'll be back in
that house, under a blanket printed with yellow sailboats.

Your mother's boyfriend, bald head ringed with red
hair, a planet on fire, kneeling

by your bed again. Air of whiskey & crushed
Oreos. Snow falling through the window: ash returned

from a failed fable. His spilled-ink hand
on your chest. & you keep dancing inside the minefield –

motionless. The curtains fluttering. Honeyed light
beneath the door. His breath. His wet blue face: earth

spinning in no one's orbit. & you want someone to say *Hey . . . Hey,*
I think your dancing is gorgeous. A two-step to die for,

darling. You want someone to say all this
is long ago. That one night, very soon, you'll pack a bag

with your favorite paperback & your mother's .45,
that the surest shelter was always the thoughts

above your head. That it's fair – it has to be –
how our hands hurt us, then give us

the world. How you can love the world
until there's nothing left to love

but yourself. Then you can stop.
Then you can walk away – back into the fog

-walled minefield, where the vein in your neck adores you
to zero. You can walk away. You can be nothing

& still breathing. Believe me.

Julia Webb

Crash Site

We remember only vaguely now the wreckage of our mother –
her damaged fuselage suspended precariously
between two broken pine trees;
how carefully one had to tread
so as not to bring the whole thing down,
and everywhere the stink of spilled aviation fuel –
at least in the beginning.

We never did find that black box
so it was always unclear exactly what had happened,
and each survivor told a different story.
But the wreckage was there for all to see –
seats and belongings scattered far and wide,
things broken open,
life jackets snagged on jagged branches.

Though our mother's windows
had popped out with the pressure,
she sometimes talked affectionately about the plummet,
but swore she could remember nothing
of our other life, before take-off.
Our first memory was the screaming of metal
and the silence which came after.

Gerard Woodward

The Fish Head

I found a fish head
With the face of Elizabeth the First
Blue blood clotted in its neck

The same look of disdain, or disgust
Or disbelief. As unloved
As anything I've ever seen.

I was in between two football pitches
In an empty playing field.
In the distance were houses,

Tiny and red like Monopoly houses.
The pitches were pricked with studmarks,
The only trace of some likely nil-nil draw.

There was other litter –
A can of Heineken, a juice carton,
A polystyrene tray faecal with

Curry sauce – in all this the fish head
Shone like a silver brooch, though it stank
And bled, still, onto my hand.

I looked up, and for the first time
Saw the common crowd,
A thousand, maybe more,

Seagulls circling in a great wheel
That seemed to hang like the roof
Of a cathedral over our suburb

Each bird playing its part as though
Toiling to move some massive structure,
Or haul in the Earth as their own catch.

Or they were watching as one eye,
A single lens focused on the severed head
I had in my hand, that one of them had found

On a shoreline, and had dropped here
Thirty miles inland. Suddenly I had them all
On a string, their centre of gravity,

Their Sagittarius A,
Daring me to put the thing down
And just walk away.

Biographies of the shortlisted writers

Forward Prize for Best Collection

Kaveh Akbar (b. 1989, Tehran, Iran) teaches at Purdue University, Indiana, and is the founding editor of *Divedapper*, a journal devoted to interviews with poets. His debut, *Calling a Wolf a Wolf*, was shortlisted for the Felix Dennis Prize for Best First Collection; *Pilgrim Bell*, his second, takes silence as part of its structure. 'I wanted the language to feel like the negative space poured around silence,' he writes. 'What's the opposite of corrosive obstinate certainty? Shutting my mouth. Letting silence sound.'

Akbar is the editor of the *Penguin Book of Spiritual Verse: 100 Poets on the Divine*, and faith of one sort or another is a constant preoccupation of his work. 'Loudly. All day I hammer the distance. / Between the earth and me. Into faith,' he writes: the unusually placed full stops, perhaps mimetic of hammer-blows, are one of *Pilgrim Bell*'s distinctive formal departures.

Anthony Joseph (b. 1966, Port of Spain, Trinidad and Tobago) is a musician and novelist as well as a poet. His work explores the transnational vibrations of the African Diaspora, 'always searching for things the language has not yet said.' *Sonnets for Albert*, his first poetry collection since 2013's *Rubber Orchestras*, is a sonnet sequence in memory of his father, by turns elegiac, deft and formally various, while remaining rooted in what is felt and tangible: 'Look out where rayo trees are planted on tumuli of bones / like ladders for spirits to cross into heaven.'

'There's an essay by Sartre in which he says that people think that language is inside of us that we have language in our brain, we possess languages and bring it out,' says Joseph in an interview with Hannah Silva. 'But Sartre says language is all around us, above us, in the air, and we pluck it out of the air, or space, and formulate it. That idea of language being outside is what I'm trying to get to, in reading the poem you access a bigger pool of language, a collective language and then words suggest themselves to you.'

Shane McCrae (b. 1975, Portland, Oregon) started writing poetry aged fifteen, having heard, 'quite by accident,' some lines from Sylvia Plath's 'Lady Lazarus': 'Those lines struck me as the gothest thing I had ever heard, and, being aspirationally a goth at the time, I immediately tried to imitate them, writing my first eight poems that day.' From these unpromising beginnings, McCrae has gone on to win a Whiting Writer's Award, a fellowship from the National Endowment for the Arts, a Lannan Literary Award, and a Guggenheim Fellowship.

Cain Named the Animals is his seventh collection, and his second to be published in the UK. He lives in New York and teaches at Columbia University. In an early review, Michael Klein observed that McCrae's poems are 'unrelenting and immediate – never delicate and never gentle.' The immediacy and relentlessness remain, but *Cain Named the Animals* is perhaps McCrae's tenderest and gentlest collection yet.

Kim Moore (b. 1981, Leicester) wrote her PhD thesis on the topic of 'Poetry and Everyday Sexism.' This creative-critical research fed into *All the Men I Never Married*. 'I know that poetry can be transformative, because it's changed my life', writes Moore, 'and I wanted to see if I could write poetry that might change or shift people's ways of thinking about sexism and gender-based microaggressions. What I didn't expect is that the writing of the book changed me – my perceptions, my understanding of sexism and its impact on me.' The poems in *All the Men I Never Married* feel like discoveries for the author, as much as for the reader.

Moore's debut collection, *The Art of Falling*, won the 2014 Geoffrey Faber Memorial Prize. She is also the author of *What the Trumpet Taught Me*, a lyric essay (like the themed sequence, a form she is drawn to) exploring her years as a music student and teacher. A second lyric essay, *Yes, I Am Judging You*, is forthcoming later this year.

Felix Dennis Prize for Best First Collection

Mohammed El-Kurd (b. 1998, Sheikh Jarrah, Occupied Palestine) 'inherited my father's stubbornness,' as he writes in 'A Song of Home.' His advice for poets starting out today is to 'be stubborn about your sentiment,' and this stubbornness in the face of settler colonialism is the central theme of *Rifqa*, named after the poet's grandmother. 'Poetry was an itch to contextualize, to inform, to hinge severed limbs onto the people to whom they once belonged, to allow those people nuance,' he writes about the early impetus behind his writing.

El-Kurd works as Palestine correspondent for *The Nation*, as well as touring and performing his poetry. 'Although this book isn't an attempt to free Palestine, its central thesis is that Palestine, in its historical entirety, must be liberated by any means necessary,' he writes in the Afterword to *Rifqa*.

Holly Hopkins (b. 1982, Berkshire) won the Poetry Business Pamphlet Competition for her debut pamphlet, *Soon Every House Will Have One*. Her shortlisted collection, *The English Summer*, is an in-depth exploration of Englishness past and present, brave, broad and resisting the counter-pressures of nostalgia and disillusion.

Hopkins' title poem 'was written while I only had time to write while the baby slept, and the baby only slept while being pushed in his pram. So I wrote it by voice-recording it on my phone in one hand, while pushing a buggy in the other. I remember the relief in having found a way to still make something.' The poem's concerns are a fine embodiment of the entire collection: 'Dun coloured endangered species of specialist interest, / best found on grungy paths, behind gabardines, / near shoes on school radiators, wet socks at work.'

Padraig Regan (b. 1993, Belfast) studied for a PhD on creative-critical and hybridised writing at Queens University Belfast, and this sense of the hybrid has fed into their work over time; *Some Integrity* combines essay (like the central 'Glitch City,' which discusses openly the animating forces implicit in some of the book's more lyrical poems) with poems responding to art and landscape, food and queer desire.

The collection's title became a guiding maxim for its assembly: 'I would only want to publish a book that had some reason for existing *as a book*, so the editorial process was mostly one of winnowing extraneous poems from the manuscript,' writes Regan. Regan has previously published two pamphlets, with Emma Press and Lifeboat, and *Some Integrity* is the 2022 winner of the Clarissa Luard Prize.

Warsan Shire (b. 1988, Nairobi, Kenya) served as the first Young People's Laureate for London, and was catapulted to global fame when she was chosen to write the poetry for Beyoncé's *Lemonade* and *Black is King*. Her journey into poetry began with a workshop at a youth centre in Northwest London, when Shire was fifteen, where she met her mentor and editor Jacob Sam-La Rose.

'On some level, I've been working on this book since 2011,' writes Shire. 'I wanted to interrogate my memories, explore childhood. I had questions, trauma I wanted to understand.' But Shire's concerns are wider than the narrowly domestic; 'Home,' with its unforgettable opening line 'No one leaves home unless home is the mouth of a shark,' universalises and makes palpable the refugee experience. (Shire wrote the short film *Brave Girl Rising*, highlighting the voices and faces of Somali girls in Africa's largest refugee camp.)

Stephanie Sy-Quia (b. 1995, Berkeley, California) grew up near Paris and studied English at Oxford. She has been writing *Amnion*, her shortlisted collection, for nine years, since she was fifteen – 'I began writing it in prose, small fragmented chunks which I didn't know how to arrange. Then, a few years in, I started putting line breaks in and suddenly it felt as if the text sighed in relief, and I remember a very clear thought of "Ah, this is what you wanted to be all along!"'

Amnion is a single long poem, exploring questions of migration, belonging and multiple origins in a form the poet and critic Kit Fan has likened to a 'detective story'; voices and themes coalesce, submerge and reunite. Sy-Quia's advice for anyone starting out in poetry today is to read omnivorously: 'Never let anyone embarrass you about what you find interesting or inspiring, and never embarrass anyone else about it!'

Forward Prize for Best Single Poem

Louisa Campbell (b. 1963, Bath) came to poetry late in life, having previously worked as a mental health nurse on acute psychiatric wards. Boatwhistle Books published her first full collection, *Beautiful Nowhere*, in 2021, following on from two pamphlets.

Her shortlisted poem, 'Dog on a British Airways Airbus 319–100', showcases her typically wry and witty approach to form, in a concrete poem reminiscent of Edwin Morgan.

Cecilia Knapp (b. 1992, Brighton) was the Young People's Laureate for London from 2020–2021. Her shortlisted poem explores her grief after her brother's suicide, finding, in Knapp's words, space for 'one aspect of grief, the surrealness and mundanity of life without the person you adored, the macabre humour we lean into to cope, the precarity of memory, the unanswerable questions you are left with.'

Knapp's debut collection, *Peach Pig*, is forthcoming this year from Corsair. Her debut novel, *Little Boxes*, was published in March by The Borough Press. In 2021, she won the Ruth Rendell Award for the writer who had the most significant influence on literacy in the UK in the previous year.

Nick Laird (b. 1975, Cookstown) lost his father to Covid-19 in March 2021. 'Up Late', his shortlisted poem, is an elegy, but also a meditation on the form of elegy itself: 'An elegy I think is words to bind a grief // in, a companionship of grief, a spell / to keep it safe and sound, to keep it // from escaping.'

Laird is Professor of Poetry at Queens University Belfast. His most recent collection, *Feel Free*, was shortlisted for the T. S. Eliot Prize and the Derek Walcott Prize. He is also a novelist, a screenwriter, and the author of a book for children about a judo-playing guinea pig, co-written with his wife Zadie Smith.

Carl Phillips (b. 1959, Everett, Washington) has published fifteen books of poetry in the USA, but it is only in the last year that he has become easily available to UK readers with the appearance of *Then the War*, his New and Selected Poems from Carcanet. This has coincided with his first appearances in UK journals, which included his shortlisted poem 'Scattered Snows, to the North.'

'It's hard to say exactly how my shortlisted poem began', writes Phillips. 'I suppose the heart of the poem is at the realization of a certain disturbing detachment of self from tenderness, regret . . . And from there, the idea that the feelings we worry about in ourselves – our helplessness – aren't just our own, these are feelings that have always existed, even back in ancient Roman times.'

Clare Pollard (b. 1978, Bolton) started writing poetry in sixth form; Bloodaxe editor Neil Astley spotted her poem 'The Heavy-Petting Zoo' in *The Rialto* and asked for a manuscript. Since then, she has published five collections with Bloodaxe, as well as a novel and a non-fiction work on children's picture books, *Fierce Bad Rabbits*.

Pollard's shortlisted poem is a deftly angled take on the pandemic and its weird reversals of emotional intuition: kindness itself becomes lethal, and accumulates indoors in drifts. 'It was best if we just locked ourselves away, / and didn't show we cared, / and hardly lived in weeks, which were our work', she writes, with an idiosyncratic and unsettling knack for putting her finger on the sore point of what she's describing.

Q&A with shortlisted writers

Each year, we ask the shortlisted poets to answer a few questions. Here's a sneak peek at the poets they admire and their advice for emerging poets. You can find the full conversations with these shortlisted poets as well as a trove of previous Prizes alumni in the library on our website at www.forwardartsfoundation.org

Which poets do you admire most and what do you value in their work?

KAVEH AKBAR

I think of Sappho, Rabia, Mahadeviyakaa, and Donne as lodestars in what silence, open breath, can do in a poem. And even Hopkins, whose staccato bombast made his silences feel so much more silent in contrast. Like the deep stillness cracking through the woods after gunshot.

ANTHONY JOSEPH

I've learned a lot from both Allen Ginsberg and Charles Olson about taking risks and listening to the voice and its slippages, also lots about the breath and how it applies to the line.

Derek Walcott and Kamau Brathwaite have both taught me about the Caribbean as a space of poetic imagination

SHANE McCRAE

Geoffrey Hill's bloody-minded intelligence helps me to keep going, though I can't keep up with it. Gwendolyn Brooks' perfect music and perfect *rightness* strike me afresh each time I read her work. John Keats' lyricism – I know that's the most boring thing I could say about Keats, but there it is – is just so hugely beautiful, and so impossible for him to restrain, that I find it exciting even when he kind of wrecks a poem with it (*cough* 'Endymion' *cough*

cough). Victoria Chang's poems surprise me constantly, and each book seems better than the one before it. Sophie Collins' *Who Is Mary Sue* is one of the best books I've read in years. The technique on display in Hannah Sullivan's *Three Poems* I cannot praise highly enough. Sasha Dugdale's hard-edged empathy! What else in poetry is like it? These are a fraction of the poets I admire most, but if I don't stop myself now I'll go on forever.

KIM MOORE

When I was writing *All the Men I Never Married* I read a lot of Maggie Nelson and Sara Ahmed so it's probably just as informed by lyric essays and academic texts than it is by poetry. But poets that I love are Moniza Alvi for her inventiveness in every collection, Liz Berry for the way she writes about motherhood and female desire, Helen Mort for the way she writes about the body and manages to use historical figures to illuminate contemporary life, Vahni Anthony Ezekiel Capildeo for the way they are so creative in their approach to their writing practice. I love Sharon Olds, Carolyn Forche, a whole host of American writers would be on my Desert Islands poem list, if there ever was such a thing. I've also just been to a reading with Mark Waldron – I love how his work treads so close to the wire of outrageousness. Clare Shaw for her use of repetition, Fiona Benson for pretty much everything that she writes – the list really could go on and on but I will stop there.

HELEN MORT

[*The Illustrated Woman*] was hugely influenced by reading Natalie Diaz and the way that she merges bodies of land and human bodies – 'merges' is the wrong word, she shows us how they are one and the same.

MOHAMMED EL-KURD

Suheir Hammad, Rashid Hussien, Aimé Césaire, Aja Monet, Audre Lorde...

PADRAIG REGAN

I love poems that resemble the structures of thinking, or that feel like the remains of a mind having worked. Anne Carson (who has discussed poetry as mimetic of thought) is a writer I feel a kind of devotion to, though I would never attempt to sound like her. I love Wallace Stephens, for similar reasons and for his 'essential gaudiness'. Ciaran Carson and Medbh McGuckian, as I mentioned, have probably been my more central 'influences'. For all their differences, what I find in both of their work is a sense of poetry as a site of infinite play, which is not foreclosed by anything as boring as 'truth'. I have also found Vahni (Anthony Ezekiel) Capildeo to be a guiding ethical example of how to write with openness to the world.

WARSAN SHIRE

There are so many poets I admire, but to name a few – Pascale Petit, Jacob Sam-La Rose, Terrance Hayes, Hiromi Ito, Ai, Idra Novey, Malika Booker, Raymond Carver, Valzyna Mort, Patricia Smith, Sharon Olds, Patience Agbabi, Kayo Chingonyi, Karen Mccarthy Woolf, Carol Anne Duffy, Nick Flynn, Jay Bernard, Andre Breton, Anne Carson.

STEPHANIE SY-QUIA

I love Anne Carson and Arundhati Roy (who is not, I realise, a poet) for their whacky senses of metaphor; Maggie Nelson for how she pole-vaults between registers; Eduardo Galeano for his books which arrange long sequences of often seemingly unrelated anecdotes; all of Michael Ondaatje's writing for very similar reasons: how he ennobles even the tiniest detail, the gentleness of his writing; Layli Long Soldier for her magnificent rebuttals to the utterances of the state. All of them operate in such a way that their writing percolates through the minds of their readers over many years, a process which for me is ongoing, and joyous. Again, also not poets, but Joan Didion and Rebecca Solnit, for their nose for the metanarrative.

But I also think it's important to think of influence in a more lateral, broad way: I love, for instance, the work of photographers Edward Weston and Imogen Cunningham, their ability to give vegetables a sense monumental scale; or how Lucien Clergue can turn a nude into something strange and playful. I can find tiny moments of cinema incredibly inspiring, and in my view some of the highest praise Amnion has received is that it contains moments of a very cinematic quality. I think cinema has an amazing capacity to ennoble, to lend a magnitude to the small, the quiet, the brief. I love that and that's what I hoped to do too.

LOUISA CAMPBELL

One of my favourite poems is 'We Think We See Richness, Said Dougal', by the inimitable Mark Waldron, a master of combining fun with the excruciatingly painful experiences of human existence in the most palatable and intriguing ways. Of course, I admire John McCullough, both for his work (that I love so much I find myself stroking the pages as I read it), but also for his persistent humility and generosity in giving encouragement and advice to less experienced poets. I love Rosemary Tonks, and wish she was still alive and writing today. My favourite poems of hers is, 'Addiction to an Old Mattress', with all its exasperation – 'Salt Breezes! Bolsters from Istanbul!' – spat out a little like the Harry Enfield character that exclaims, 'Poisonous Monkeys!'

CECILIA KNAPP

Too many to list! Caroline Bird taught me about finding the joy in writing, the impossibility of what we do and how that can be ultimately freeing and generative. Rachel Long gave me permission to say the things in poems I thought I 'wasn't supposed to say.' Natalie Shapero is endlessly hilarious and devastating. Gboyega Odubanjo is a delight to read and watch; his voice is compelling and original. I always go back to James Tate and Frank O'Hara and Anne Carson. Lately I've enjoyed reading Hannah Sullivan, Jack Underwood and Rachael Allen – the contemporary poetry community is just abundant with brilliant, distinct voices.

NICK LAIRD

There's so many, but looking at my shelves, and sticking only to the non-alive: Bishop, Auden, Yeats, Eliot, Amichai, George Herbert, Zbigniew Herbert, Dickinson, Wordsworth, Issa, Wallace Stevens, Whitman, Rilke, Louise Bogan, Thomas Wyatt, Heaney, Walcott, MacNeice, Kavanagh, Derek Mahon, CD Wright, Szymborska, Jane Kenyon, Etheridge Knight, Andrew Marvell, Keats, Norman MacCaig, Basho, Larkin, Berryman, Les Murray, Nicanor Parra, Donald Hall, Lucille Clifton, Thomas Campion, Rumi, Sylvia Plath, Paul Valery, Philip Levine, Larry Levis, Nazim Hikmet, Cavafy, Transtromer, James Dickey, Catullus, Mahmoud Darwish, Robert Herrick, Mary Oliver, Georg Trakl, David Berman, Lucie Brock-Boido, Carlos Drummond de Andrade, Horace, Akhmatova, Robert Frost, DH Lawrence, Ashbery, Frank O'Hara, James Tate, Rosemary Tonks, Ted Berrigan... I could go on a long time. Emperors have their treasures, and we have ours.

I admire different things in different poets – but if you're intent on distinguishing principles, I respond to a facility with language, something surprising and yet inevitable in the work, and strength of voice, of tone.

CARL PHILLIPS

Such a hard question! I should start by saying I'm most drawn to poetry that makes me see the world anew and as if for the first time, shaking up my assumptions about the world. And I especially like it if I'm made to think differently about language itself. I love the syntax and penetration of thought in Jorie Graham's work. I love the mystery and the bridging of past and present in Eiléan Ní Chuilleanáin's poems. I love the formal dexterity and the interrogation of eros in Thom Gunn's work. Robert Hayden and Rita Dove are two poets whose work showed me that to be a Black poet didn't mean I had to write toward anyone's expectations. There's often a pressure on Black poets to write about race and to do so in a specific way. I have long argued for what I call a politics of mere being – of being who we are, in all of our fullness, which means

I get to write about race, walking my dog, being queer, Roman empire, whatever I choose to. Dove and Hayden's poems were crucial models of that for me.

CLARE POLLARD

Too many to mention, really. John Donne was my first passion, and Sylvia Plath and Anne Sexton had the biggest influence on me, when I was forming as a poet. So, I love the really brilliant image-makers.

Ovid, obviously, for the dramatic monologues. Frank O'Hara is my favourite love poet. Adrienne Rich was a huge influence on my last book, *Incarnation*, as a writer who is both intimate and very political. As are Gwendolyn Brooks and Wanda Coleman, both poets I've been going back to a lot.

Of our contemporaries: Anne Carson, Maria Stepanova, Carolyn Forché, Kim Hyesoon, Marie Howe, Ilya Kaminsky, Natalie Diaz.

What advice would you give to anyone starting out in poetry today?

KAVEH AKBAR

Be deeply skeptical of anyone living, including me, who gives prescriptive advice, including this! Wislawa Szymborska, from a late interview: 'I've reached the age of self-knowledge, so I don't know anything. People who claim that they know something are responsible for most of the fuss in the world.'

ANTHONY JOSEPH

Establish a daily writing practice. Read as much as you can. Read and follow references, from one poet to the next. Read some more. Read 'contagious' poets like Kamau Brathwaite, Anne Sexton and Nick Makoha, learn by emulating them, fall in love with the melody of their word music.

Immerse yourself in the community of poets, go to events, join groups, go to readings, support other poets.

SHANE McCRAE
Read. Read everything. Read poets who came before you at least as frequently and with at least as much attentiveness as you read your peers. Read even – especially! – poetry you don't feel you understand, and allow yourself not to understand it. Allow even not understanding to be joyful.

KIM MOORE
Enjoy starting out. You'll never be starting out again! And read lots of poetry – not just collections, but anthologies and journals if you can. Read much more than you write – reading solves most problems.

HELEN MORT
Read. And never stop reading. You can always learn more from other poets. Don't ever think your work is done!

MOHAMMED EL-KURD
Write for people. Not for prizes or platitudes. Not for poets discussing your words around their workshop tables. Write as if your poems are open homes. And be stubborn about your sentiment.

HOLLY HOPKINS
Find other people who enjoy writing, whose work you admire and who will be honest with you.

PADRAIG REGAN

I wouldn't want to presume that any advice I may give would be useful, especially to a general 'anyone'. There are as many ways to go about writing poetry as there are people writing poetry, so I think advice is probably best when it is bespoke.

WARSAN SHIRE

If this is a dream of yours, I'm proud of you for following your dreams. We need to find out what's available to you – workshops, masterclasses, look online, local libraries, youth centers, council funded spaces, poetry journals, mentoring programmes. Read well and often. Read everything. Write everyday, release the steam. Keep writing until you find your voice. Take good care of yourself. Theres no rush. Don't give up.

STEPHANIE SY-QUIA

Be omnivorous: don't just look to other poets or writers. Look broadly for other sources of influence and don't be a snob. Never let anyone embarrass you about what you find interesting or inspiring, and never embarrass anyone else about it! Also: find out what it is that you do for rest and play. Don't be afraid to let the fields of the mind lie fallow.

LOUISA CAMPBELL

Firstly, be yourself! Use *your* words; *your* voice. We already have a Seamus Heaney, a Wayne Holloway-Smith, an Ilya Kaminsky, and they're superb, but we haven't yet heard [insert your own name].

If you're writing just for yourself, be as self-indulgent as you like. Writing a poem is a wonderful way to vomit difficult emotions out of your mind and onto the page. I've found it incredibly helpful for working through anger, which is often a tricky old emotion to express. Sometimes writing a poem's like sorting out your underwear drawer. It starts off an unruly mess spilling out over the edges, but once you've tidied it, everything fits and the drawer closes.

If you want your work published, you need to be looking at what you've written and thinking why should someone use minutes of their life they'll never get back to read it? What's in it for them? Will they learn something? Will it give them little happy mind spangles? Will it make them laugh, or cry (in a good way)?

And this is a biggie for me (which seems obvious, but I had to hear it from Liz Berry before the penny dropped): if you want your poem published, only submit it to magazines you really love, not to those you think you 'ought' to get into.

In fact, forget 'ought' altogether; it's a ghastly concept.

CECILIA KNAPP

Don't be afraid to write about the things you want to, in a voice that feels right for you. And have fun. Don't take it too seriously. That's when the magic happens.

CARL PHILLIPS

Well, I know this is what everyone says, but my top advice is to read as widely and variously as possible – that's how you learn about language's capabilities, how things have been done, how they have been done differently, and how people have thought about things over the centuries. Reading is often where my poems will start, often something as simple as encountering a word in a novel, say, that I've never thought to use. I'll write that word down and save it for a poem draft later. Many of my poems begin with my riffing on a word or phrase I've encountered elsewhere.

The other piece of advice is just as obvious, but crucial, I think: Look closely at everything around you. When I'm disappointed in a poem I've read, it's often because the poem doesn't seem to take place in the actual world of human life. I think of writing poetry as a form of world-building. Which means, to me, that a poem should be more than one person's private thoughts. Where is the thinker? What do they perceive? Are there trees? Is a loaf of bread being baked and the smell filling the house? Does the thinker have a body? For me, poetry begins with keen attention. And then the challenge is to use language, not to transcribe what we take in from the world, but to transform it. To leave the reader as changed as the writer has been changed.

CLARE POLLARD
Only write the poems you have to write. Submit to *Bad Lilies*.

Publisher acknowledgements

Kaveh Akbar · Reza's Restaurant, Chicago, 1997 · Reading Farrokhzad in
   a Pandemic, *Pilgrim Bell* · Chatto & Windus
Qudsia Akhtar · My Dad is a Terrorist · *Khamoshi* · Verve Poetry Press
Will Alexander · extract from *Refractive Africa* · Granta
Claire Askew · Foreplay · *How to Burn a Woman* · Bloodaxe
Polly Atkin · Monthlies · *Much with Body* · Seren
Sheri Benning · plainsong · *Field Requiem* · Carcanet
Fiona Benson · Edelweiss · *Ephemeron* · Jonathan Cape
Emily Berry · Scholar · *Unexhausted Time* · Faber & Faber
Clíodhna Bhreathnach · *Aughrim Street Doomscroll* · Banshee
Sam Buchan-Watts · Lines following · *Path Through the Woods* · Prototype
Victoria Adukwei Bulley · Declaration (I) · *Quiet* · Faber
Louisa Campbell · Dog on a British Airways Airbus 319–100 · *Perverse*
Joe Carrick-Varty · From the Perspective of Coral ·
   The Manchester Review
Anne Carson · Theseus [voiceover] · extract from *H of H Playbook* ·
   Jonathan Cape
Maya Caspari · Mixed Other · *The Poetry Review*
Anna Cheung · Monster Tinder · *Where Decay Sleeps* · Haunt Books
Rohan Chhetri · King's Feedery · *Lost, Hurt, or In Transit Beautiful*
   · Platypus
Carolyn Jess Cooke · Things Will Work Out · *We Have to Leave the Earth*
   · Seren
Alex Dimitrov · Sunset on 14th Street · *Love and Other Poems* · Corsair
Mohammed El-Kurd · Boy Sells Gum at Qalandiyah · Bulldozers
   Undoing God · *Rifqa* · Haymarket
Mark Fiddes · Hotel Petroleum · The Moth Poetry Prize
Jay Gao · Imperium Abecedarian · *Imperium* · Carcanet
Louise Glück · Poem · *Winter Recipes from the Winter Collective* · Carcanet
Roz Goddard · Small Moon Curve · The Moth Poetry Prize
Hannah Hodgson · What Happened? · *163 Days* · Seren
Holly Hopkins · Telephone Girls · Explanation for Those Who Don't
   Know Love · *The English Summer* · Penned in the Margins
Sarah James · Marcasite · *Blood Sugar Sex Magic* · Verve Poetry Press

Anthony Joseph · Jogie Road · Breath · *Sonnets for Albert* · Bloomsbury

Cecilia Knapp · I'm Shouting I LOVED YOUR DAD at my Brother's
Cat · *Perverse*

Lisa Kelly · Red Data List of Threatened British Fungi: Mainly Smuts ·
PN Review

Zaffar Kunial · The Wind in the Willows · *Magma Poetry*

Nick Laird · Up Late · *Granta*

Mukahang Limbu · The Day · *Oxford Poetry*

Fran Lock · Hyena Q & A · *Hyena! Jackal! Dog!* · Pamenar Press

Amelia Loulli · Holy Water · *Under the Radar Magazine*

Lila Matsumoto · All of the pans in the kitchen · *Two Twin Pipes Spout
Water* · Prototype

Shane McCrae · Eurydice on the Art of Poetry · The Butterflies the
Mountain and the Lake · *Cain Named the Animal* · Little Brown

Lucy Mercer · Imago · *Emblem* · Prototype

Kim Moore · When you rewind what happened... · Is it rape... · *All the
Men I Never Married* · Seren

Jake Morris-Campbell · Each Pebble Its Part · *Corrigenda for Costafine
Town* · Blue Diode Press

Helen Mort · A Well-known Beach · Loch Allua · *The Illustrated Woman* ·
Chatto & Windus

Briancia Mullings · Queen's Speech · *The Poetry Review*

Molly Naylor · The Worries · *Whatever You've Got* · Bad Betty Press

Eiléan Ní Chuilleanáin · What happened next? · *Poetry London*

Eugene Ostashevsky · We are trying to make sense (published as 4) ·
The Feeling Sonnets · Carcanet

Stuti Pachisia · Boys Over Flowers · *The Rialto*

Mark Pajak · The Tilt · *Slide* · Jonathan Cape

Anita Pati · Train Triolet (16.46 to Brighton) · *Hiding to Nothing* ·
Pavilion Poetry

Carl Phillips · Scattered Snows, to the North · *PN Review*

Claire Pollard · Pollen · *Bad Lilies*

Ayesha Raees · When I was a child... (published as 38) · *Coining a
Wishing Tour* · Platypus Press

Padraig Regan · 50ml of India Ink · Salt Island ·*Some Integrity* · Carcanet

Denise Riley · Tick tock · *Lurex* · Picador

Denise Saul · Golden Grove · *The Room Between Us* · Pavilion Poetry

Peter Scapello · Nerve · *Limbic* · Cipher Press

Elisabeth Sennitt Clough · The Black Dress · *The Cold Store* ·
    Pindrop Press

Warsan Shire · Bless Grace Jones · Midnight in the Foreign Food Aisle ·
    Bless the Daughter Raised by a Voice in Her Head · Chatto & Windus

Greta Stoddart · Flowers for my ego and a dark stage · *Fool* · Bloodaxe

Stephanie Sy-Quia · extracts from *Amnion* · Granta

Anastasia Taylor-Lind · Welcome to Donetsk · *One Language* ·
    Poetry Business

Olly Todd · Tides · *Out for Air* · Penned in the Margins

Jessica Traynor · Anatomy Scan · *Pit Lullabies* · Bloodaxe

Ocean Vuong · Tell Me Something Good · *Time Is a Mother* ·
    Jonathan Cape

Julia Webb · Crash Site · *The Telling* · Nine Arches Press

Gerard Woodward · The Fish Head · *The Vulture* · Picador

Winners of the Forward Prizes

Best Collection
2021 · Luke Kennard · *Notes on the Sonnets* · Penned in the Margins
2020 · Caroline Bird · *The Air Year* · Carcanet
2019 · Fiona Benson · *Vertigo & Ghost* · Cape Poetry
2018 · Danez Smith · *Don't Call Us Dead* · Chatto & Windus
2017 · Sinéad Morrissey · *On Balance* · Carcanet
2016 · Vahni Capildeo · *Measures of Expatriation* · Carcanet
2015 · Claudia Rankine · *Citizen: An American Lyric* · Penguin Books
2014 · Kei Miller · *The Cartographer Tries to Map a Way to Zion* · Carcanet
2013 · Michael Symmons Roberts · *Drysalter* · Cape Poetry
2012 · Jorie Graham · *PLACE* · Carcanet
2011 · John Burnside · *Black Cat Bone* · Cape Poetry
2010 · Seamus Heaney · *Human Chain* · Faber & Faber
2009 · Don Paterson · *Rain* · Faber & Faber
2008 · Mick Imlah · *The Lost Leader* · Faber & Faber
2007 · Sean O'Brien · *The Drowned Book* · Picador Poetry
2006 · Robin Robertson · *Swithering* · Picador Poetry
2005 · David Harsent · *Legion* · Faber & Faber
2004 · Kathleen Jamie · *The Tree House* · Picador Poetry
2003 · Ciaran Carson · *Breaking News* · The Gallery Press
2002 · Peter Porter · *Max is Missing* · Picador Poetry
2001 · Sean O'Brien · *Downriver* · Picador Poetry
2000 · Michael Donaghy · *Conjure* · Picador Poetry
1999 · Jo Shapcott · *My Life Asleep* · OUP
1998 · Ted Hughes · *Birthday Letters* · Faber & Faber
1997 · Jamie McKendrick · *The Marble Fly* · OUP
1996 · John Fuller · *Stones and Fires* · Chatto & Windus
1995 · Sean O'Brien · *Ghost Train* · OUP
1994 · Alan Jenkins · *Harm* · Chatto & Windus
1993 · Carol Ann Duffy · *Mean Time* · Anvil Press
1992 · Thom Gunn · *The Man with Night Sweats* · Faber & Faber

Best First Collection
2021 · Caleb Femi · *Poor* · Penguin Books
2020 · Will Harris · *RENDANG* · Granta

2019 · Stephen Sexton · *If All the World and Love Were Young* ·
  Penguin Books
2018 · Phoebe Power · *Shrines of Upper Austria* · Carcanet
2017 · Ocean Vuong · *Night Sky with Exit Wounds* · Cape Poetry
2016 · Tiphanie Yanique · *Wife* · Peepal Tree
2015 · Mona Arshi · *Small Hands* · Pavilion Poetry
2014 · Liz Berry · *Black Country* · Chatto & Windus
2013 · Emily Berry · *Dear Boy* · Faber & Faber
2012 · Sam Riviere · *81 Austerities* · Faber & Faber
2011 · Rachael Boast · *Sidereal* · Picador Poetry
2010 · Hilary Menos · *Berg* · Seren
2009 · Emma Jones · *The Striped World* · Faber & Faber
2008 · Kathryn Simmonds · *Sunday at the Skin Launderette* · Seren
2007 · Daljit Nagra · *Look We Have Coming to Dover!* · Faber & Faber
2006 · Tishani Doshi · *Countries of the Body* · Aark Arts
2005 · Helen Farish · *Intimates* · Cape Poetry
2004 · Leontia Flynn · *These Days* · Cape Poetry
2003 · AB Jackson · *Fire Stations* · Anvil Press
2002 · Tom French · *Touching the Bones* · The Gallery Press
2001 · John Stammers · *Panoramic Lounge-Bar* · Picador Poetry
2000 · Andrew Waterhouse · *In* · The Rialto
1999 · Nick Drake · *The Man in the White Suit* · Bloodaxe Books
1998 · Paul Farley · *The Boy from the Chemist is Here to See You* ·
  Picador Poetry
1997 · Robin Robertson · *A Painted Field* · Picador Poetry
1996 · Kate Clanchy · *Slattern* · Chatto & Windus
1995 · Jane Duran · *Breathe Now, Breathe* · Enitharmon
1994 · Kwame Dawes · *Progeny of Air* · Peepal Tree
1993 · Don Paterson · *Nil Nil* · Faber & Faber
1992 · Simon Armitage · *Kid* · Faber & Faber

Best Single Poem
2021 · Nicole Sealey · Pages 22–29, *an excerpt from* The Ferguson
  Report: An Erasure · *Poetry London*
2020 · Malika Booker · The Little Miracles · *Magma Poetry*
2019 · Parwana Fayyaz · Forty Names · *PN Review*
2018 · Liz Berry · The Republic of Motherhood · *Granta*

2017 · Ian Patterson · The Plenty of Nothing · *PN Review*

2016 · Sasha Dugdale · Joy · *PN Review*

2015 · Claire Harman · The Mighty Hudson · *Times Literary Supplement*

2014 · Stephen Santus · In a Restaurant · Bridport Prize

2013 · Nick MacKinnon · The Metric System · *The Warwick Review*

2012 · Denise Riley · A Part Song · *London Review of Books*

2011 · RF Langley · To a Nightingale · *London Review of Books*

2010 · Julia Copus · An Easy Passage · *Magma*

2009 · Robin Robertson · At Roane Head · *London Review of Books*

2008 · Don Paterson · Love Poem for Natalie "Tusja" Beridze ·
The Poetry Review

2007 · Alice Oswald · Dunt · *Poetry London*

2006 · Sean O'Brien · Fantasia on a Theme of James Wright ·
The Poetry Review

2005 · Paul Farley · Liverpool Disappears for a Billionth of a Second ·
The North

2004 · Daljit Nagra · Look We Have Coming to Dover! ·
The Poetry Review

2003 · Robert Minhinnick · The Fox in the Museum of Wales ·
Poetry London

2002 · Medbh McGuckian · She Is in the Past, She Has This Grace ·
The Shop

2001 · Ian Duhig · The Lammas Hireling · National Poetry Competition

2000 · Tessa Biddington · The Death of Descartes · Bridport Prize

1999 · Robert Minhinnick · Twenty-five Laments for Iraq · *PN Review*

1998 · Sheenagh Pugh · Envying Owen Beattie · *New Welsh Review*

1997 · Lavinia Greenlaw · A World Where News Travelled Slowly ·
Times Literary Supplement

1996 · Kathleen Jamie · The Graduates · *Times Literary Supplement*

1995 · Jenny Joseph · In Honour of Love · *The Rialto*

1994 · Iain Crichton Smith · Autumn · *PN Review*

1993 · Vicki Feaver · Judith · *Independent on Sunday*

1992 · Jackie Kay · Black Bottom · Bloodaxe Books

Supporting Poetry with Forward

In buying this book you have helped Forward support new talent, engage young people and build poetry's audience. Thank you!

Forward was founded to showcase the best new poetry and to build bigger, more diverse audiences for poetry. Our aim was to focus on the *new*, to share contemporary lived experience through poetry. After three decades, that's still at the heart of what we do.

The Forward Prizes are the most influential awards for new poetry published in the UK and Ireland, and since 1992 have lauded some of the most recognised names in poetry alongside the most exciting emerging voices.

Our books include *Poems of the Decade*, now on the A-Level syllabus. Each October National Poetry Day generates an explosion of activity in communities nationwide, with thousands of amazing events – on doorsteps and at kitchen tables, in gardens and streets, in schools, libraries and public spaces both online and offline – all proving poetry's power to bring people together. In all, our work reaches around 1.2 million people each year.

We are ambitious for poetry's future and work in partnership with publishing, arts, education and community organisations to have the biggest impact. We want to enable more poets, potential poets and poetry lovers to create an artform that is relevant and representative of the UK today.

To find out more how you can support us and get involved in our work, please email lucy@forwardartsfoundation.org or get in touch on Facebook or Twitter @ForwardPrizes